# MARKETING
# PLANS IN ACTION

# MARKETING PLANS IN ACTION

## A STEP-BY-STEP GUIDE
for Libraries, Archives, and Cultural Organizations

Franklin Lakes Public Library

AMANDA L. GOODMAN

**ALA**
Editions

CHICAGO 2019

**Amanda L. Goodman** is the publicity manager at Darien Library, a public library in Connecticut. Prior to this role, she was the user experience librarian there. Goodman is the author of *The Comparative Guide to WordPress in Libraries: A LITA Guide* (2014) and the *Library Technology Report* "Digital Media Labs in Libraries," and she has written for *UX Magazine*, *Library Journal*, and *Public Libraries Magazine*. Her projects include cofounding LibUX (https://blog.libux.co), creating a worldwide map of 3D printers in libraries, and teaching classes on WordPress, UX, and digital signage. Goodman is serving as a LITA Board director-at-large for 2017–2020.

© 2019 by Amanda L. Goodman

Extensive effort has gone into ensuring the reliability of the information in this book; however, the publisher makes no warranty, express or implied, with respect to the material contained herein.

ISBN: 978-0-8389-1812-8 (paper)

**Library of Congress Cataloging-in-Publication Data**

Names: Goodman, Amanda L., author.
Title: Marketing plans in action : a step-by-step guide for libraries, archives, and cultural organizations / Amanda L. Goodman.
Description: Chicago : ALA Editions, 2019. | Includes bibliographical references and index.
Identifiers: LCCN 2018051699 | ISBN 9780838918128 (print : alk. paper)
Subjects: LCSH: Libraries—Marketing—Handbooks, manuals, etc. | Archives—Marketing—Handbooks, manuals, etc. | Marketing—Management—Handbooks, manuals, etc. | Marketing—Data processing—Handbooks, manuals, etc.
Classification: LCC Z716.3 .G66 2019 | DDC 021.7—dc23
LC record available at https://lccn.loc.gov/2018051699

Cover design by Alejandra Diaz. Image © Adobe Stock.

♾ This paper meets the requirements of ANSI/NISO Z39.48–1992 (Permanence of Paper).

Printed in the United States of America

23 22 21 20 19    5 4 3 2 1

**we are for each other**

—E.E. Cummings

*In memory of Celeste.*

# contents

# preface

I WAS A USER EXPERIENCE LIBRARIAN WHO WAS GIVEN A NEW CHARGE TO manage my public library's marketing needs. My reaction to this was to balk. I am a librarian, not a marketer. The only directive given to me was to formalize the library's publicity workflows. At the time, I did not understand the overwhelming size of this task. It was hidden by its scattered nature, with each department doing their own thing when it came to marketing. Then the day came when I took on my new responsibilities, and I wished I knew where to start. The anxiety of that day has inspired this book.

When I checked the marketing landscape, I could not find anything on how to set up my processes or what to consider. Instead, there were only tips on writing marketing plans. When staring at the blank calendar ahead of me, those tips were meaningless. I managed to pick myself up, learned about our existing marketing workflows, and then worked to create more efficient ways to do things. As a culmination of my process, I created the succinct and specific guides in chapters 2–10 of this book. If you're new to the job, like I was, this book will get you through some anxious moments and help you make sense of your role. More experienced library marketers will find guides to help you complete more tasks.

I draw from lessons I have learned as a publicity manager in a public library. Each guide in this book is a faithful explanation of what I have done to make my own work easier. While I draw from personal experience, my goal is for these guides to help you manage any aspect of marketing work in a library, archive, or other cultural organization. Since few marketers in libraries are devoted solely to one job, this book allows you to implement only the strategies that meet your current needs.

Technology changes frequently. Therefore, I do not give explicit instructions for what to do with any software or on any website. Instead, I present the overall picture, explaining the concept to you, and suggesting the functionality to look for in order to complete the task.

The director of marketing at the publisher Houghton Mifflin Harcourt, Carla Gray, uses a ship metaphor to describe her role in the workplace: "I've always thought of the marketing role as the cruise director; involved in the whole book's life, and responsible for coordinating with all departments to ensure smooth sailing."[1]

In that spirit, I hope this book will help you become the cruise director of your organization's marketing efforts.

## NOTE

1. Kimberly Burns, Whitney Peeling, and Michael Taeckens, "Ask the Publicists: What's the Difference between Marketing and Publicity?" 2017, https://lithub .com/ask-the-publicists-whats-the-difference-between-marketing-and-publicity.

# acknowledgments

I WAS WARMLY WELCOMED TO MARKETING BY KATE PETROV OF THE GREENWICH Library in Connecticut. She invited me over and gave me permission to ask her whatever I wanted to know. Thank you, Kate. You provided a kindness which I will never forget.

My colleague Virginia Grubbs has a background in marketing. We've spent many hours working on projects together, learning from each other, and trying our best to get stories published in the local papers. She is a gem without equal.

Liz Sisemore of Texas State University reviewed the structure of the guides in this book and gave me some much appreciated feedback. Her advice led to my rearranging the organization of the guides' content and adding time to complete a task as a factor to consider.

Towards the end of writing, I sought advice on the structure of the book. My thanks to Frank Skornia, Rachael Clark, Mark Aaron Polger, Kathy Dempsey, and Theresa Cahill Agostinelli. They helped me think it through so I could finish the book on time.

Writing a book means you miss out on adventures with loved ones. The patient understanding of Celeste, Chii, Thomas, PK, and Jessica made every word in this book possible.

*chapter* 1

# Getting Started

CONGRATULATIONS ON YOUR NEW ROLE! YOU MAY HAVE SOME PREVIOUS experience with promoting your organization's resources and services to your users. Or maybe your administration has decided to get serious in sharing the organization's good work with the public and has reassigned you to this new role. Or maybe marketing has been added to your already overflowing plate. Either way, you need some help.

This book is intended to help relieve your stress, get your priorities in order, and establish a smooth marketing system. Most of the techniques discussed in this book can be accomplished with no money. However, I recommend asking for an allowance so you can splurge on small items to make your life easier (e.g., pre-made graphics).

You can read selections from this book in any order, depending on where you are in your marketing role. If read straight through, this book will guide you in setting up systems that you can set in motion and let run. Once you have these systems in place, you can then focus on your day-to-day tasks without worrying about whether you missed some deadline somewhere. You will already have that deadline documented and scheduled, and you will have time enough to work on it.

This book skips heavy marketing and project management theory. The guides consist of two types: practical step-by-step tutorials, and concept explanations. The latter teach ideas you need to consider and how to integrate them into your work.

So set aside an hour each day to read this book and learn something new. By the end of the book, your work life will be so routine that you can start proposing more ambitious marketing projects. Your boss will be impressed.

# What Is Marketing?

Marketing is the name of the overarching field that you will be working in. The Chartered Institute of Marketing in the United Kingdom defines marketing as three key areas:[1]

- Identifying something that people or businesses want and are prepared to pay for, or a problem that they would like solved . . .
- Developing a product or service . . . which meets that need, and then promoting that product or service so that the audience is aware of its existence.
- Working out the details and making sure you're charging the right price for the product or service.

For your organization, pricing may not apply directly. However, you are often asking your users to invest some amount of time and effort in interacting with your library's resources, events, and services. If that amount is too high, they'll go elsewhere.

The key thing here is to find out what your users want and then figure out how to let them know that your organization can help them fulfill that need just when they're looking for help. Of course, sometimes people are not looking for anything with a specific goal in mind, so you will also spend time just keeping them aware of what resources and services your organization has to offer.

## MARKETING VS. PUBLICITY

There is no clear, set answer as to what defines marketing versus publicity. There are disagreements across the board on the scope and limitations of these two areas, so I will set my own limits. Publicity is a specific subfield of marketing which focuses on specific campaigns. Marketing is a broader term that encapsulates all of your efforts to let users know that you have something they want or need. The term you use may mean something specific within your organization, but overall, both of these terms are used to mean any efforts to bring attention to something you have to offer users. The terms marketing and publicity are somewhat interchangeable in casual, everyday use. Marketing may be considered a term that is too commercial for some nonprofits. Nevertheless, in this book, I will use the term marketing.

## CAMPAIGNS

In this book, the word campaign is primarily used to refer to e-mail marketing efforts. An individual e-mail that you send from your service provider of choice (MailChimp, Constant Contact, Emma, etc.) to many users is known as a campaign.

You may also refer to a marketing push for a specific goal as a campaign. Most such campaigns are short-term efforts that wrap up over the course of a few weeks. Alternatively, a campaign may be a year-round effort. Your preferred terms for all such efforts can be interchangeable. Different software, marketing books, and blogs vary in their terminology.

# A Word on Titles

### JOB TITLES

My job title is publicity manager. I researched the titles of similar positions in comparable industries and found a broad range in use. When it was settled upon, the important term was manager, since I am the project manager and oversee all of my library's marketing efforts.

Your job title can be any one or a combination of these terms: publicity/marketing manager, outreach coordinator, manager of marketing services, marketing campaign manager, brand manager, digital librarian, manager of communications, marketing analyst, manager of public relations, or even audience engagement coordinator. New trends will emerge and other job titles will develop in the future.

For this book, I will refer to you as a marketer.

### DO I NEED A DEGREE?

No, you don't need a degree to be a marketer, but depending on your organization, it may be helpful to have a degree in marketing or communications. In February 2018, Tammie Evans asked the members of the Facebook group Library Marketing and Outreach (LMaO) which degrees they had.[2] Of the 491 respondents, 49 percent said they had a library degree.

Your local colleagues in other organizations may differ. For example, all of the library marketers I have met around my county (in Connecticut) have marketing degrees. I was the unusual one without a formal marketing background. However, I do urge you to flip to Guide 33: "Educational Resources" to see some easy-to-access educational resources that can help you expand your skill set.

### WHAT TO CALL THE END USER

There is a lot of disagreement about whether you should use the terms patron, user, customer, client, end user, and so on in defining the people you wish to communicate with. Since I have a user experience (UX) background, the term I use in this book is user.

# Where Do You Fit in the Organizational Structure?

When I was asked to take over marketing in my library, I was granted the freedom to define my job and my title. Since this was a new role for the library and I had no formal marketing background, I needed to learn what marketing looked like in other organizations.

I started by going to Google and researching the titles and job duties of similar positions in libraries, cultural organizations, nonprofits, and corporations in recent job ads. Of the ten positions I evaluated, four were listed at the management organizational level, three reported to a director, and three ads gave no indication of where the job fit within the overall structure. The marketing person was usually part of the administrative team. To try this exercise for yourself, check out Guide 2: "Outline Your Job Scope."

At my library, I stayed within the UX department for a year before transitioning into the adult programming department. After this move, I was concerned at first that other departments thought I represented only my own area's interests instead of the whole library. Thankfully, as things turned out, that concern never became an issue. What I learned is that you can do marketing from wherever you are within the overall structure of the library. By taking the responsibility to be transparent and fair in managing concurrently running promotions, my worries about favoritism never came to pass.

## Document Everything

### DECISIONS

As your library's marketer, you will be making a lot of decisions, setting up workflows, and developing policies in the months to come. When you look back at it, you will want to know why you made such-and-such a decision and when you made it. If you include your reasoning, you will be able to evaluate your past decisions against new knowledge or technologies to see if you should revisit any of these issues. For example, perhaps that automated text messaging system you wanted two years ago is now possible. By keeping your list of decisions written down and located in a central place, you can answer any questions that may arise in the future.

It's also helpful to just keep track of your ideas. Which ones worked? Which did not and why? What did you investigate to solve the issue? Bonus: This list is also useful for future job interviews. You will be able to easily give examples about a time you succeeded (or failed) at a task.

Check out Guide 14: "Internal Tracking System," for examples of how to set up this internal tracking system for your decisions and ideas.

### PERSONAL KNOWLEDGE BASE

You also want to develop a personal knowledge base for yourself and your successor. You can use this to document how to do everything for your job. For example, who are the outside contacts who will use your press releases in their publications (Guide 59: "Document Your Public Relations Contacts")? How often do you contact them? Check out Guide 13: "Personal Knowledge Base" for what to consider when setting up your knowledge base.

## The Buck Stops Here

### TAKE RESPONSIBILITY

As the marketer, you need to take responsibility for your actions and those of your colleagues. Any publicity that the organization puts out—in any format and by anyone—is seen to be done by the institution as a whole. Mistakes will be made. In the best of circumstances, you can correct a typo by editing or deleting a post immediately after publication. However, if it's been up there for a while and someone mentions it, you have to own it. If you are lucky, you can make amends to the commenter with humor (and maybe a GIF), and the user will feel heard, and their positive feelings about you will strengthen. Evaluate the situation with care.

Warning: If your organization has committed a serious offense or breach of etiquette, do not use humor.

The best defense against making a mistake and then needing to apologize is to be careful and thoughtful right from the start. Ask a colleague to look over anything that will be printed or e-mailed—because you cannot fix it once it's been sent out. Read your tweets aloud to yourself to catch any typos or grammatical errors. If anything gives you pause, double-check it with someone else and explain why you are hesitant. You don't want to be too careful, but you should try to avoid any obvious land mines before they go out.

## CULTURAL SENSITIVITY

This is one part of the job which is difficult. You will need to continuously educate yourself on which terms, ideas, and associations may cause distress or emotional pain to your users (and yourself).

### Words

Phrases that were commonly used in the past may be recognized today as a slur. Often the terms or ideas were always harmful, but it was not until recently that many people have become aware of their darker undertones. Widespread awareness of these issues comes up on a regular basis, so you need to be on top of what may cause offense. If you have moved any distance for your job, you may come across offensive words or phrases that you have never encountered and do not recognize as such. In these cases, listen to your gut and pay attention. If anything triggers a slight doubt, double-check it with a trusted and socially conscious colleague.

### Co-Opted Ideas

An innocent idea, image, or topic can sometimes be co-opted by individuals and given an ugly association. The Pepe the Frog meme of a cartoon frog was originated in 2006 by Matt Furie.[3] Nevertheless, the meme was appropriated in 2016 as a hate symbol, as documented by the Anti-Defamation League.[4] As an avid Internet user, I was familiar with the meme, but I had never seen it in its negative incarnation until Hillary Clinton's campaign brought widespread attention to it. Part of your job as a marketer is to keep an eye out for when ideas, phrases, or topics turn negative. You will also need to train your colleagues on these issues. Some issues will be self-evident, but as with Pepe the Frog, you need to pay attention to them on an ongoing basis.

Warning: Actively seeking to learn about harmful ideas and expressions can take a toll on your mental health. Take care of yourself. I pick up my knowledge by following conversations on Twitter, Tumblr, and national news outlets, so the discussions on those forums explain the issues, and I don't have to view active harassment.

### Remain Vigilant

Other occasions when your organization can inadvertently cause offense are selections promoted for a history month or awareness campaign. For example, if you are showing films for Women's History Month, stick to films that are about real women instead of animated fairy tales. If you choose a film which has a dark theme like domestic violence, you may want to accompany this film with a group discussion about the topic afterwards. For these kind of themed promotions, try to ask a member of that group to check the list of selections. It may turn out that a particular movie is perceived as troubling within that group.

### Resources

- Anti-Defamation League, "Hate on Display™ Hate Symbols Database," www.adl.org/education-and-resources/resource-knowledge-base/hate -symbols
- Anti-Defamation League, "Anti-Bias Tools and Strategies," https://www .adl.org/education/resources/tools-and-strategies/anti-bias-tools-strategies
- Southern Poverty Law Center, "Hate and Extremism" guide https://www .splcenter.org/issues/hate-and-extremism

## APOLOGIZE

If a mistake is made in a marketing effort, your organization needs to take action. A well-written policy will give you guidelines on how to approach the issue. Depending on the severity of the mistake, you may respond in larger or smaller ways.

If you are in a top-level managing position that only reports to the director or the board, you will likely be the one to handle the complaint. If you are at a lower level, your immediate boss may oversee the process. Regardless, you should work with your colleagues on a collaborative approach to handle the situation. With many perspectives, you can assess how to handle the complaint in the most effective way.

Note: Your policy needs to cover how to handle comments which may be accusatory or inflammatory. See Guide 68: "How to Apologize" for tips on addressing apologies, and Guide 67: "Handling Complaints" for handling complaints.

# Welcome to the Guides

The seventy-two guides in this book will help you get started on your marketing work. You can read them in any order as needed. The time estimates in these guides are well-padded. The difficulty level in the guides is set with the expectation that you are familiar with computers and the Internet. It is recommended that you read Guide 1: "Getting Staff Buy-In" first. This will help you to understand how marketing already works in your organization, and your role in improving it, and it will help you to start building good rapport with your colleagues.

The guides are written in two formats: step-by-step tutorials and explanation guides.

## TUTORIALS

By following a tutorial, you will be guided through a project with a definite outcome of data-gathering, building a workflow, or establishing relationships. The tutorial offers tips on how to expand a project and which things to keep in mind. If applicable, things to watch out for close out the tutorial.

## EXPLANATIONS

Sometimes a tutorial guide is not the right way to learn about a topic. There may be too many complications or things to consider which cannot be boiled down to a simple "do this, then that" guide. The explanation guides will go over what you should know, what you should consider, and the ways to proceed for a given topic. You will gain a basic understanding of the factors surrounding a topic, so that you know what to learn more about if it applies to your situation.

## NOTES

1. Chartered Institute of Marketing, "Get into Marketing," https://www.cim.co.uk/more/get-into-marketing.
2. Tammie Evans, Library Marketing and Outreach's Facebook page, 2018, https://www.facebook.com/groups/acrl.lmao/permalink/1700249466681142.
3. Imad Khan, "4chan's Pepe the Frog Is Bigger Than Ever—and His Creator Feels Good, Man," 2015, https://www.dailydot.com/unclick/4chan-pepe-the-frog-renaissance.
4. BBC News, "Pepe the Frog Meme Branded a 'Hate Symbol,'" 2016, https://www.bbc.com/news/world-us-canada-37493165.

*chapter* 2

# Learn about Your Organization

**IF YOU ARE JUST STARTING YOUR MARKETING JOURNEY, THIS ENTIRE CHAPTER** will help you understand your job better, obtain staff support, and learn about your organization. The most important guide in this chapter is Guide 1: "Getting Staff Buy-In." If your colleagues don't understand what it is that you do and how you will be supporting their work, the rest of your job will be an uphill battle.

## GUIDE 1: Getting Staff Buy-In

### YOUR GOAL

The perception of what marketing is doing for your organization can look great to one person but look terrible to another. The staff may also feel unheard and stressed by trying to do marketing on their own when they're pressed for time or they lack the necessary know-how. Moreover, you won't know what their particular needs are and what has or hasn't worked in the past (from their perspective) unless you ask them these things. By doing in-depth interviews with staff members, you can learn a lot about how your organization really works and your role within it. You will walk away from these meetings with solid ideas and tips for how to make everyone's jobs easier.

### DIFFICULTY LEVEL

This task may take an emotional toll on you if the staff are especially stressed or if they are especially frank and candid with you.

**TIME** It will take a lot of time to set up the interviews with staff members, attend all of these 60- to 90-minute meetings, write up the data, analyze it, and then form plans of action.

**COST** Free.

**WHAT YOU NEED TO START** Learning about your organization's needs will take a while to do. You will need time to set up interviews, conduct them, document your findings based on them, and follow up on what you've learned.

**TOOLS**
- E-mail or phone to schedule interviews
- Calendar to track interviews
- Space to meet
- Note-taking items

**STEPS**
1. Draft an e-mail invitation to department heads to meet with you to discuss marketing. They can bring whomever they'd like to the meeting.
2. Outline your goals, and ask them the following questions:
   a. Who are the audiences you are targeting?
   b. What marketing materials do you need?
   c. Who makes those materials?
      - Follow up with these people to find out what tools they use to make the materials.
   d. How far in advance do you know about your promotional needs?
      - Advance notice can vary across projects; for example, paid speakers may be booked months in advance, while a book display can be decided upon today.
   e. When is the latest you get information or items from outside partners?
   f. What are your promotional trouble spots?
   g. What do you want me to do for you?
3. At the meeting, explain that you want to learn how marketing has been done, what issues have gotten in their way, and what would make their work easier. Let them know that their answers are confidential and no private details will be shared. Mean this.
4. Listen, ask questions to clarify things you don't understand, and take detailed notes. Resist the urge to contradict, though if you have knowledge, clear up any misconceptions which can help open up the conversation.
5. After the meeting, type up your notes. Clearly mark things which cannot be done and note why. You can add these to your personal knowledge base (Guide 13) or internal tracking system (Guide 14).

6. Share your notes with the department. Exclude any comments which should be held in confidence.

7. When all meetings have concluded, analyze everyone's concerns and ideas. For things that can be done, start scheduling out time blocks to work on addressing those issues by learning more about them and developing solutions (Guide 8: "Time Management").

8. Share your list with your supervisor as needed and work through the list of action items.

9. In six months, e-mail the departments individually to let them know how you have addressed their concerns and what you will work on in the next six months. Let them know if any of their requests turned out to be something that cannot be done.

10. Follow up in another six months. You may want to schedule another round of interviews in order to see how things have changed in the past year.

   • Note: Staff may be less candid now than they were before. However, you have hopefully built trust with them and they will be honest.

**TIPS**
Be humble and open while listening.

Bonus of this activity: Getting staff buy-in will help you feel better about the work you're doing, and it is useful for your annual review.

**WATCH OUT!**
Take the promise of keeping confidential comments private to heart. You don't want to cause harm to your colleagues by sharing these comments with anyone else. Exclude them in your typed-up notes. The comments provide you with background knowledge of how things became the way they are. Use this information wisely and learn from it how to do better.

## GUIDE 2: Outline Your Job Scope

**YOUR GOAL**
In project management, you have to watch out for "scope creep" in which the project goes beyond the original plan. Likewise, your job can quickly start adding on extra duties. These extra tasks may not be accompanied by additional manpower or a decrease in other responsibilities. To keep your sanity, outline what you will be in charge of and stay reasonably rigid about its boundaries.

**DIFFICULTY LEVEL** Intermediate.

**TIME** Up to two hours.

**COST** Time.

**WHAT YOU NEED TO START**
You should have talked to your supervisor in order to gain an understanding of the needs of the organization. How will your role help support the organization's mission?

**TOOLS**
- Spreadsheet
- Word processor

**WHAT YOU NEED TO KNOW**
If you are lucky enough to be able to define your job, you may run into pushback on where you draw the line when it comes to taking on extra duties. Or maybe *you* need to be realistic about what you can manage to do in the time you have available to work.

**STEPS**
1. As described in chapter 1, in the section "Where Do You Fit in the Organizational Structure?" one way to discover what your role should be responsible for is to research similar positions in job ads. Look not only within your own industry, but also in parallel ones, and even in the corporate world.
    - To look at parallel industries means that if you work in a library, look at archives and museums.
2. Create a spreadsheet with columns to track the position description and job duties listed in the ads. Place an X in the column if the area was mentioned (see the *Website to Video* columns in the list). The columns should be as follows:

    a. Job Title
    b. Organization Level
    c. Website
    d. Social Media
    e. E-Mails
    f. Press Releases
    g. Graphic Design
    h. Video
    i. Other Duties
    j. Place
    k. URL (where you found the information)

3. Look again at the ads and pull out things that are of interest to you. Copy these into a document.
4. Based on the needs of your organization, the job duties mostly commonly cited, and the tasks of interest, write your own job description.
    - Use the template your organization already uses.

- Or use this sample template:
  a. Job Title
  b. Job Description
  c. List of Communication Venues (newspapers, social media, signage, etc.)
  d. Organizational Level/Placement
  e. Evaluation Criteria for Success

5. Your job scope is now defined as to which tasks you will handle and which ones fall outside of your domain. For example, you may post content to social media, but you are not expected to be the graphic designer.

6. If you cannot handle some tasks, you may be able to compensate for this by finding public domain, Creative Commons, or free items online (e.g., photos).

**TIPS**

Find out whether you have the final say in most communication matters or not. You want to establish if you are responsible for all the publicity the organization produces or not. These areas are defined as anything posted online, printed, and recorded. If you are responsible for everything, include a statement to that effect in your job scope. Then start brainstorming the checks and balances that will help you maintain order across the organization. For example, if you write an e-mail newsletter, it needs to be proofread by someone else (and vice versa).

Establish who has ultimate authority in contentious matters. This may be the director or the board. Hopefully, their input will rarely be needed.

**WATCH OUT!**

If you are unable to handle an aspect of the job (e.g., filming and video editing), let your supervisor know up-front. Ask to have time and resources to study the topic. Perhaps a colleague can help you out.

Be careful not to make yourself the sole set of eyes for everything that goes out. You have other tasks to do and will need help. Work with individual departments to set up a point person in their group who will inspect the work going on there (Guide 35: "Staff Training Now and in the Future"). If this person has questions, they can then bring them to your attention. You want to try and avoid having to inspect every post about an event or program if it can be double-checked at a more local level.

## GUIDE 3: Know Your Branding

### BRANDING

Since your organization has recognized the importance of marketing, they may already have some branding in place. This may include a logo, color schemes, and a document outlining which words they use and avoid, and how to write things (e.g., e-book vs. eBook). If your organization has no branding in place, check out Elisabeth Doucett's book *Creating Your Library Brand: Communicating Your Relevance and Value to Your Patrons.*

Before we go any further, what is branding? The American Marketing Association defines a brand as a "name, term, design, symbol, or any other feature that identifies one seller's good or service as distinct from those of other sellers."[1] As a cultural organization, your library is probably not selling products per se, but you do want your audience to think of it as a distinct entity compared to others like it.

Branding also involves the way people *feel* about your organization. Do they tell everyone about their latest visit or book they got from you? Or do they complain about the lack of parking? This all adds up to part of your branding. So branding is more than just a logo or your marketing material. However, for our purposes, we'll focus on what you can have an impact on.

### COMMON BRANDING ELEMENTS

It will make your marketing life easier if your organization has these elements on hand:

- Logo: Get a vector (i.e., an endlessly resizable) version and one with a transparent background.
- Color schemes: These are usually pulled from the logo and are complemented with a few other acceptable colors.
- Font: Go open source if you can. Otherwise you are on the hook to pay for every license for each computer the font is installed on.
- Voice and tone: Are you friendly? Serious? Do you use GIFS or crack jokes?
- Writing guidelines: Let everyone know you wrote this text.

### CONSISTENCY IS KEY

You can define your branding elements, but they will not acquire instant recognition value unless they are used consistently. As the head of marketing, you need to insist that everyone work within your branding guidelines.

I always think of Target, the department-store retailer, as my ideal brand guru. They stick strictly with their red-and-white motif. If you see their logo, it is always red. Then I think of their fun commercials from the early 2000s. They found creative ways to use their red-and-white color scheme and logo in each commercial. It's all over their stores. This is consistent branding.

Now think about your own organization or a neighbor's building. How often do you find a flyer or sign that is outside the branding colors? You don't have to take your branding to the extent that Target does, with most commercial models only wearing red or white. However, your logo, fonts, and the feel of your marketing material should say *this is us.*

## VOICE AND TONE

Along with visual representation, your organization needs to define how it "speaks." This includes not only the images you use in your marketing, but also how you write things, or respond on social media. If your organization only uses Victorian-era images in your materials (think Trader Joe's), then it may be off-brand to post selfies on social media.

To figure out your organization's voice and tone, talk with your colleagues, director, and users and note what comes to mind when they are asked to describe your organization. Develop just a few keywords that emphasize who you are *and* what you aspire to be. Then stick with these when creating marketing content. For example, Trader Joe's marketing can be described as quirky, funny, and light-hearted.

A great primer on these concepts is MailChimp's Voice and Tone (https://styleguide.mailchimp.com/voice-and-tone) guide. This popular e-mail marketing platform has made its voice and tone guidelines public. Then take it up a notch by reading the book *Nicely Said* (www.nicelysaid.co), cowritten by MailChimp's communication director, Kate Kiefer Lee.

## WRITING GUIDELINES

You can be strict with your writing guidelines, or you can just hammer home a few key points for staff to remember. For most organizations, you should keep your guidelines to a page or two. Your writing guidelines may include:

- How to write the organization's name: The Cool Archive or just Cool Archive
- Do you ever drop portions of the name and write "The Archive is open . . ."?
- Which words do you use (e.g., e-book vs. digital book)?
- Which words you never use
- How to write certain words (e.g., checkout or check out)

## LOGO USE

Your logo brings its own challenges. For your nonmarketing colleagues, all this branding stuff can seem inane. However, you are trying to build up a consistent look and feel and trigger instant recognition among your users when they encounter your materials. Some decisions to make regarding your logo are the following ones:

- Who may use the logo in their materials?
- Should the logo be on marketing materials?
- Where do you store the logo for easy access?
- Can the colors be changed for different occasions (e.g., pink for Valentine's Day)?
- If your logo is dark and the background is dark, do you have a light version? And vice versa?
- Can you add a drop shadow to your logo to make it stand out?

Make sure to have your logo in a variety of sizes and formats. When you work with vendors, they will ask for your logo in a variety of shapes (square, rectangle), sizes, with and without transparent backgrounds, and print or web quality. You don't have to make all these up-front as long as you have the original high-quality file. When a request comes in, you can make the logo that is needed and add it to your logo folder.

## COLORS

When deciding on the colors of your organization in your materials, document them in RGB (screen), CYMK (print), and Pantone codes. This comes in handy when you are special-ordering marketing materials. If you do this work up-front, it will save you time later on when you have a last-minute rush request. Be aware of Pantone colors: they don't always match exactly to the color you intended. In these cases, choose whatever is closest. There are converters online to help you find the Pantone color if you enter the CYMK values.

## PUT IT ALL TOGETHER: STYLE GUIDE

Once you have all these common branding elements decided upon, write them down. You can go simple and just create a text document which includes images to illustrate your points. Or you can build a browser version. See Brad Frost's boiler-plate template (http://bradfrost.github.io/style-guide-guide/). The middle ground is a beautiful document such as the United Kingdom's National Archives branding guidelines.[2]

There are hundreds of examples of branding guides online. They go by many titles based on the industry (style or identity guides). So pick out some big companies you like and start searching for their guides. If you can get permission, you can publish yours as well online. It's always interesting to see what other cultural organizations are doing.

## ENFORCING BRANDING

The tricky part in all this branding is that just because you create a guide and document it, that doesn't mean that anyone in your organization will actually use it. Someone is always going to go rogue and just print out a Comic Sans "out of order" sign. *Breathe.* Try to nip these derelictions in the bud before these bad habits start to spread. Some strategies to help are the following ones:

- Get your supervisor's 100 percent support of the brand guides and enforcement.
- Memorize an elevator pitch on why branding is important.
- Insist on meeting all new staff and going over the brand guidelines if there's any chance they may make a sign (Guide 35: "Staff Training Now and in the Future").
- Have some examples of your branding to show what good adherence to the guidelines looks like (this may already be in your guide).

- Make sure your documentation of the guides is easily accessible to all staff.
- If you are just starting out, go to department meetings to introduce and explain the new branding guides.
- Have answers ready for those who just want to do their own thing.
- If you have strict requirements for something, stay on top of it. If someone messes up, make them correct it. Be nice about it (use a sympathetic but firm tone), but insist that the infraction has to be fixed.
- Try to head off the staff's impulse to create noncompliant "out of order" signs by making some and laminating them. Place them at the locations where staff may be tempted to make their own. Work with their department head to insist that the pre-designed signs be used.

In my experience, if you have a strict requirement and are careful to enforce it, colleagues will quickly default to following the rules. This is especially true if they have to redo the work themselves. It's an awkward moment to confront them, but you want people to self-regulate themselves. If you are just starting this strict policy, within a couple of months, you should be able to ease up on actively watching for slipups. Colleagues now know that you will make them fix the work, which can be a huge time drain on them. It's better for them to do it right the first time.

Likewise, if you don't stay on top of enforcement of your guidelines, one person going off the rails will lead others astray. This is especially true in naming files in a central repository (Guide 18: "File Management"). If someone starts naming or organizing files wrong, within a short time you may see others following their lead. Then you will be stuck trying to untangle who did what and making them change it. People can be especially resistant to fixing their errors if you let these slip by for months.

### Resources

- Jackson Walters, *Breakthrough Branding: Positioning Your Library to Survive and Thrive* (Chicago: ALA Neal-Schuman, 2013).
- Lisa A. Wolfe, *Library Public Relations, Promotions, and Communications: A How-To-Do-It Manual for Librarians*, 2nd ed. (Chicago: ALA Neal Schuman, 2005).

### NOTES

1. American Marketing Association, AMA Dictionary.
2. United Kingdom, National Archives, "Explore Your Archive Campaign Toolkit: 03 Brand Guidelines," 2016, www.nationalarchives.gov.uk/documents/archives/explore-your-archive-toolkit-3-brand-guidelines.pdf.

# chapter 3

# Get Notified of Marketing Requests

ONE OF YOUR MAJOR TASKS IS TO TAKE CONTROL OF THE MARKETING OUTput for your organization. In order to do this, you will need to know what marketing offerings you have available and develop ways to gather requests from colleagues for marketing tools or campaigns through the use of an e-mail or a standard form.

Once you have set up a system for your colleagues to ask for your help, you will also need ways to keep track of your own work. The personal knowledge base and internal tracking system will help you remember why you did things and how you are doing from year to year.

## GUIDE 4: Make an Inventory of Marketing Offerings

**YOUR GOAL**
Regardless of whether your duties include creating original content or designs, you will need to know what marketing materials you can offer your colleagues. New ideas will come up as new software, products, services, and funding become available. Creating this inventory will clarify the ways you might expand your organization's marketing output.

**DIFFICULTY LEVEL** Easy to intermediate.

**TIME** Two hours.

**COST** Free.

## WHAT YOU NEED TO START

If you've been at your organization for a while, you are probably aware of its traditional marketing methods. If you're new, you will need to ask what has been done, the standard workflow (in-house vs. hired designers), and the budget.

## TOOLS

- Spreadsheet

## STEPS

1. Start by making a spreadsheet with these columns:
   a. Item
   b. Format
   c. Creators
   d. Tools Used
   e. Costs
   f. Estimated Time
   g. Notes

2. Create a list of all the marketing items you can find within the building and online. These may include flyers, bookmarks, social media, press releases, and e-mail newsletters. Look for anything that your organization uses to get the word out about its resources, services, or programs.
   - Note the item's format as digital, physical, or audiovisual.

3. Write down who makes these items in each department.

4. What tools are used to create these items (e.g., Adobe Photoshop, Publisher)?
   - Note: You may not be able to answer this question until you ask all of the departments who creates their area's marketing (Guide 1: "Getting Staff Buy-In").

5. What costs are associated with this item? Printing, outside design work, staff development time?

6. How long does it take to make an average item of this type?
   - You may not know this at the start. Overestimating the time is recommended.

7. Share this spreadsheet with your supervisor to look for any items that should be added or removed.

8. This spreadsheet is just for the eyes of you and your supervisor. Make a simplified version with only the format types for your colleagues. Use this spreadsheet as a basis for your ingest form, in which your colleagues submit their requests for promotional help (Guide 7: "Ingest Form Setup").

**TIPS**

This inventory list is a bit of a brain dump that helps you understand your position better. If you know which staff create marketing materials, you may be able to rely on them to help with future projects (Guide 32: "Build a Network of Support"). Finding out or guessing how long it takes to create specific items will help your time management (Guide 8: "Time Management").

You should collect various examples of marketing items so you can see what materials have been produced in the past. You can use these for inspiration, to discover blind spots or design issues, to look for patterns, or to help build your organization's branding documents (Guide 3: "Know Your Branding"). Place these items aside for now. Taking photos of them is a space-saving method of achieving this tip.

Over time, you can add new marketing output items to your list as you gain more confidence and understand your audiences better. For example, if your organization was paper-only, you can explore adding digital marketing forms, like social media posts. This inventory list will not change too much over time.

It's handy to memorize what you can offer so you can quickly answer questions with authority. Marketing is your domain. Own it. Know what you are capable of doing.

**WATCH OUT!**

If a marketing item is only used for special purposes (e.g., an annual report sent to a designer), you may not want to include it on the list you share with your colleagues. Items of this caliber are often out of reach for most promotions due to their associated costs.

This inventory document is flexible. You can phase out current offerings and add new ones.

## GUIDE 5: How to Gather Marketing Requests

**YOUR GOAL**

How will your colleagues submit their requests to you for promotional help? You can set up a strict system that relies on either e-mails or ingest forms to submit requests. (An *ingest form* is also called a *submission form*.) This guide details the differences in these two different workflows for submitting requests, and how to choose the one which works best for you.

**DIFFICULTY LEVEL** Easy.

**TIME** Thirty minutes.

**COST** Free in most cases.

**WHAT YOU NEED TO START**
E-mail or online form creation software.

**WHAT YOU NEED TO KNOW**
The decision about which system to use will affect your colleagues' overall impression of your marketing efforts. If the one you choose doesn't work for how you do things, you will have difficulties in meeting your colleagues' needs, especially when you stop following the system you set up. Select your workflow carefully to avoid this catastrophe.

**PROS AND CONS OF E-MAIL**
- It is easier to e-mail someone than to bookmark a link to a form.
- E-mails can be organized automatically by developing a tag or folder system (Guide 18: "File Management").
- All contacts with colleagues are kept in your e-mail, which is probably where most of your work communications are already stored anyway.
- It is not easy or is impossible to annotate a submission by e-mail.
- Confusion and mix-ups can occur depending on your e-mail's search capabilities and how subsequent e-mails are handled (e.g., nesting or threaded e-mails).
- Tracking new additions to a request is harder when using e-mail.
- Requesters can forget details, and you will need to follow up for more information.

**PROS AND CONS OF INGEST FORMS**
- The ingest form's fields help the requester add all the pertinent details which they may forget in an e-mail.
- The ingest form's text is saved as a spreadsheet.
- It is easy to sort rows in the form in order to see who is making requests and when.
- The ingest form's fields can be updated, and notes can be added, such as due dates and when you followed up on the request.
- All ingest form requests are saved together, which helps you evaluate and analyze overall requests.
- Ingest form submissions are often sent to you as e-mail notifications. The formatting can make it difficult to read.
- An ingest form takes more time to set up.
- Spreadsheets may be difficult to read for long text entries.

**TIPS**
You can choose to use both methods. Be clear about which projects should go through the ingest form and which ones can be e-mailed to you. Simple requests such as social media promotions for an under-registered event can be done through e-mail. More complex projects with multiple marketing items should go through an ingest form, if you allow both contact methods.

Your ingest form spreadsheets can be sorted to help you develop a year-round calendar of requests in order to look for patterns of slow and busy times. See Guide 30: "Calendars to Develop" on what calendars you can develop.

If you choose an ingest form, you can avoid looking at a spreadsheet altogether by just gathering the request and entering it into your project management system (Chapter 4: "Set Up Project Management").

**WATCH OUT!**

If you allow staff to submit requests outside your system, you open yourself to overlooking or missing requests or deadlines by you or the requester.

## GUIDE 6: E-Mail System Setup

**YOUR GOAL**

You prefer to keep all communications in one place, so all marketing requests will come to you via e-mail. This guide shows you how to use folders, labels, and hierarchies to manage your e-mails.

**DIFFICULTY LEVEL** This is easy if you are familiar with e-mail folders or tagging systems.

**TIME** Thirty minutes.

**COST** Free.

**WHAT YOU NEED TO START**

E-mail account.

**TOOLS**

- E-mail account
- Web browser for research

**WHAT YOU NEED TO KNOW**

These particular steps depend upon your e-mail client of choice (e.g., Apple Mail, Gmail, Hotmail, Outlook, or Yahoo!).

- If you are using Gmail, you *label* (tag) your e-mails.
- If you are using the others, you sort your e-mails into *folders*.

The difference is that a single e-mail goes into one folder. With labels, you can put multiple labels on a single e-mail (e.g., Mom, Sister, and Travel for an e-mail about your summer travel plans with your family members).

Many people prefer not to sort their e-mail, just archive it, and keyword search it later. This is a valid choice, but this guide helps you to be more organized. Specific steps for your e-mail client are not included here, since the steps may change before this book goes to print.

**STEPS**

1. Do a web search for the name of your e-mail client and *label* or *folder*, depending upon your e-mail client (e.g., *Gmail labels*).
    - If *folder* does not show up your e-mail client, try *label*.
2. Look for the latest guide on how to add labels or folders in your e-mail client. Follow those steps to create either folders or labels.
3. Also look up *subfolders* and *nested labels*. These will help you group your e-mails into smaller categories for even better organization.
    - Note: Not all e-mail clients have supported this feature.
4. Suggested folders or labels which may or may not apply to your situation:
    - Establishment Meetings (Guide 1: "Getting Staff Buy-In")
    - Big Programs
        - [Name of recurring annual program 1]
        - [Name of recurring annual program 2]
    - Education
    - Ideas
    - Press Releases (Guide 62: "Press Releases")
        - PR Inbox to Do
        - Sent PR
        - Published PR
        - E-Mails to PR Contacts
    - Permissions
    - Printed Projects (sent out to a professional printer)
        - [Name of recurring annual print job 1]
        - [Name of one-off professional print job]
    - Requests (Chapter 3: "Get Notified of Marketing Requests")
    - Social Media
    - Stats
    - Video
    - Web

The sections below give further details on specific folders/labels.

### Education

This is a catch-all for any e-mail tutorials, links, and resources to help you get better at your job.

### Ideas

If you collect your ideas for new projects or new approaches by e-mailing yourself the idea, you can store those e-mails in here. You may also gather these in analog format, in spreadsheets, or with an app. This folder helps you keep track of your own initiatives—which is great for your performance review.

### Press Releases

If you will be e-mailing your local public relation contacts, you need to keep track of all those e-mails.

- The *Inbox* is used if your colleagues send you press releases (PR) to send out on their behalf.
- Once you have sent all the press releases in that e-mail, move the e-mail from the *Inbox* to the *Sent PR* folder.
- The *Published PR* folder is useful if you receive/send only a single press release per e-mail. After you see that a press release was selected for publication, you can move it to this folder from the *Sent PR* folder. This is just one way to help you keep track of your success rate if you don't want to do so in a spreadsheet.
- The *E-Mails to PR Contacts* is for when you have non-press release reasons to write your contacts (e.g., asking a question or setting up a meeting; see Guide 60: "Set Up Meetings").

### Permissions

If your policies require you to get permissions from users, content creators, or others, keep all of those e-mails in here. The term *content creators* refers to anytime your organization asks permission to use an item (e.g., a photo) that was created by someone else.

### Requests

Since you have decided to accept marketing requests from your colleagues via e-mail, you need a place to collect them all (Guide 18: "File Management"). You can add subfolders/nested labels for different people, projects, or departments. I recommend you don't make a folder for *every single* project, just ones big enough to warrant lots of e-mails back and forth.

### TIPS

There are add-ons which can help you organize your e-mail into folders *or* tags. One example is EmailTags for Outlook (https://www.standss.com/emailtags/default.html). However, it is easier to work within the organizational system you already have, instead of spending time looking for ways to change it. Choosing add-ons adds a technical burden on you to make sure the add-on remains compatible with your e-mail client in the future.

You can set up rules or filters to automate your processes. For example, e-mails from a marketing educational newsletter can be automatically sorted into the Education folder (Guide 33: "Educational Resources").

### WATCH OUT!

Don't create too many folders or labels at the outset. You'll learn over time which folders or labels work best for your needs. Add more as you need them.

## GUIDE 7: Ingest Form Setup

**YOUR GOAL**

You want marketing requests to come in pre-organized, with the content entered into the ingest form's fields to ensure that you get all the information the first time. Depending on the software, ingest forms may be stored in a spreadsheet, a CSV file, a database, or in an e-mail.

**DIFFICULTY LEVEL** Intermediate.

**TIME** Sixty minutes.

**COST** Free for most users.

**WHAT YOU NEED TO START**

The list of questions that staff should answer on the ingest form.

**TOOLS**

- Web-based form software such as Airtable, Google Forms, JotForm, or Wufoo

**WHAT YOU NEED TO KNOW**

Consider which questions are required information each time. The name of the point person would always be needed. If a field isn't needed every time, don't make it required on the ingest form.

**STEPS**

1. Log into your web form software and create a new form.
2. At the top, include a text box (usually HTML) which contains a short explanation of how much in advance you want to be alerted about projects (Guide 5: "How to Gather Marketing Requests").
   - If you have some flexibility in your schedule for easy, last-minute projects, note that here.
3. Consider if you will need conditional logic in your form (see the "Tips" section below).
4. Add fields for each question you want to ask. Field types differ to help make form creation and submission easier.
   - See the "Tips" section (below) for explanations of common fields.
5. Questions you may wish to ask with suggested field type:
   - Point Person [short text]
     - Note: The submitter may not be the responsible party.
   - Name of Project [short text]

- Event/Project Description [long text]
- Theme and Design Ideas [long text]
- Website URL of post if available [URL]
- Marketing Items to Be Developed [table]
    - More information on this is in the "Tips" section.
- Is another organization(s) cosponsoring this event or program? [radio buttons]
    - Yes
        - This shows "Who are our cosponsors?" in a long text field if selected.
    - No
- Any other comments? [long text]
- Want an in-person consultation? [radio buttons]
    - Yes
    - No
- Attach supporting images or documents. [upload]
6. Set up how you want to be notified of new submissions. E-mail alerts is the easiest way.
7. Look carefully over any additional fields that your software supports. You may have options to:
    - Show or e-mail the submitter a confirmation message.
    - Create a custom confirmation message.
    - Choose someone else to receive the e-mail (e.g., the web designer rather than the social media person).
8. Test the ingest form out yourself and with the help of at least one other person. You want to make sure it is clear, easy to understand, and everything works properly.
9. If you run into trouble, check the form creator's support forums or submit a ticket (as applicable).

**TIPS**
Bookmark the link to the ingest form on your colleagues' computers to make it easy for them to access the form.

**Conditional Fields**
When choosing your form software, get one with conditional logic. That way, you can hide unnecessary fields if they do not apply to this submission. For example, if a questions asks about cosponsors, and they select no, the field "Who are our cosponsors?" will remain hidden. If they select yes, a hidden field asking the name of the cosponsoring organization will be shown.

Conditional fields are also great for automatically routing submissions to the correct person. This will save you time because you no longer have to forward submissions yourself. However, not all form software offers this feature. JotForm.com is one that does, as of this writing.

## Common Field Types

- Checkboxes: These allow for a multiple-choice option. Don't mix these up with radio buttons.
- Date and time: For selecting when.
- Drop-down menu: This is good for questions like state of residency, but it has accessibility concerns because it is difficult for some people to use.
- E-mail: This only accepts complete e-mail addresses with @ signs.
- Header or HTML: Only you can add text to this field. It allows you to break up the appearance of the page, highlight different segments, and enter long explanations and instructions.
- Long text: This is for the user to submit longer explanations and descriptions.
- Name: This usually asks for the first and last name as separate fields which are grouped together.
- Number: This is if you are looking for a number-only answer. Be clear if the currency or percent signs are already figured into the field.
- Phone number: This is to add consistency to the entry of phone numbers. No more missing area codes!
- Radio button: This shows multiple options but allows for only one selection.
- Short text: This is for just a few words.
- Table: This allows you to ask for information and the due dates for particular marketing pieces.
- Upload: This allows the user to attach documents, images, audio, or videos.
- URL: This is for website addresses. It often requires *http://* or *https://* at the front.

## Table Field

For an ingest form, you want a table that lists all of the marketing items that you can support (Guide 4: "Make an Inventory of Market Offerings"). Your rows would be a list of all the marketing items. Your columns may be:

- Date the item will go out (e.g., 7/28/2019)
- Who is making the item?
- Do you need help in making it?

As of this writing, Google Forms does not support custom text input in its table (grid). Instead, it only offers checkboxes or radio buttons.

*Bonus Fields*
- Intended Audience [checkboxes]
    - General Interest
    - Parents and Caregivers
    - Kids
    - Teens
    - Workers/Business
    - Seniors
    - Other
        - This shows a short text field if selected.

- Would you like this event to be filmed or photographed?
    - Note: Only if your organization supports this capability.

- Will you be serving food and/or drinks? [radio button]
    - Yes
        - What will you serve? [long text]
    - No

*Special Field Types*
Your form may support uncommon fields like "select answer by clicking on images." In JotForm.com, this is known as the Image Picker field. There are dozens of other special field types that can be used to great effect. For your ingest form, you will probably not need anything too unusual.

*Resources*
- Luke Wroblewski, *Web Form Design: Filling in the Blanks*

**WATCH OUT!**
Make your ingest form as simple and straightforward to use as possible. Avoid using marketing jargon.

# chapter 4

# Set Up Project Management

YOU HAVE A LOT OF THINGS TO KEEP TRACK OF IN YOUR WORK. HOW ARE YOU going to do it without forgetting anything? Enter your project management (PM) setup. The options for this system include digital and paper-based systems. With this system, you will be able to track your own projects and knowledge, make publicity plans, and strategize for the future. This chapter concludes with an explanation of how a marketing request is handled within my own PM setup.

## GUIDE 8: Time Management

**YOUR GOAL**
How long will it take you to do things? How far in advance do you need to be notified of marketing needs? What happens if someone has a last-minute request?

**DIFFICULTY LEVEL** Intermediate.

**TIME** Two hours minimum.

**COST** Free.

**WHAT YOU NEED TO START**
It is helpful to know what your weekly repeating tasks are before you start. Do you have a public-facing desk shift in your library? Do you have weekly meetings with

colleagues, department heads, or your supervisor? You should also know what your job responsibilities are at this point (Guide 2: "Outline Your Job Scope").

## TOOLS
- Calendar or planner
- Paper or spreadsheet

## WHAT YOU NEED TO KNOW
The steps below will enable you to see how your time is accounted for before you even get to your "free time." Then you will make guesstimates on how much time it takes to do non-weekly tasks. The time estimates are based upon my own experiences. You should adjust them to meet your own needs.

The system below is aimed at those who closely monitor their time by blocking it out on a calendar.

## STEPS
### *Figure Out Your Schedule*
1. In your calendar, block out the hours for tasks that happen each week.
   - Take your list of job duties and reduce them to simple terms like "meeting with supervisor," "social media," "press release," and so on.
2. Include your lunch period for each day, and breaks if applicable.
3. If e-mail is a big part of your job, block out an hour each day for it.
4. I recommend you keep an hour free every day for last-minute requests. If nothing happens, it gives you time to work longer on other projects, answer more e-mails, or get started on the next day's tasks.
5. Write down your monthly tasks as well.
   - Your first week of the month may be filled with gathering stats, writing reports, and attending meetings.
6. Look at your calendar and think about when you are most alert during your workday. You will want to schedule more mentally challenging tasks during those periods.
7. Pulling from your list of job duties, write down estimates of how long it takes to do each of those tasks (in their most general form, like social media).
8. Pad your time out:
   - If you expect to take 30 minutes to do something, write down 60 minutes.
   - If you need to do research, add another 30 minutes.
   - If you need to write a report, expect to take 60 minutes to do this.
   - If you need to use unfamiliar software and learn how to use it, quadruple your time.

- For graphic design projects like posters, flyers, or bookmarks, plan for 1 to 2 hours.

9. The goal is to overestimate, so you can then deliver earlier than expected, to the delight of your colleagues.
   - Always expect to be interrupted. Padding your time up-front allows you to work around those interruptions.

10. Ask how far in advance the notice of different types of projects, events, and services has been given or advertised in the past. Ask if those time lines seem to be effective.

11. Find out the turnaround time for items to be published or scheduled to go up (e.g., digital signage).

### Learn Other People's Schedules

1. Take note of when regularly scheduled promotions are sent out from your organization.
   - If an events e-mail is only sent out once a month during the first week, you will need to get everything ready before that date, or else you'll miss your chance.

2. If you need to submit marketing items to newspapers, blogs, radio, printers, or other venues, make sure you know how far in advance they need their materials (Chapter 9: "Outside Contacts").

3. Consider how far in advance your colleagues get materials (e.g., headshots, biographies) from their event presenters. You will use those materials to promote the event.
   - You may need to build in some flexibility for these outside partners. An event can start being promoted weeks before a headshot is submitted.

### Build Out Your Calendar

1. Once you have estimates and requirements from others, you can start planning how far in advance you need promotional materials submitted to you. Think in terms of when the submitter requires the item to go out for distribution. Work backwards from there to establish the bare minimum date.
   - For example, a flyer which is designed and printed in-house may need to be distributed two weeks before the event. So then you need to consider how long it will take to be designed, double-checked for errors, and printed. At the earliest, then, you could say three weeks before the event date. However, you should pad your time. Remember that you may have other projects pop up.

2. Be diligent to enter all your project time lines into a calendar. If it is a repeating task each week or month, you may be able to automate that as a repeating event, so that you don't need to manually enter it each time.

3. If you use a digital calendar to keep track of your time, you can easily move tasks around to accommodate new tasks as they come up.

4. Periodically remind your colleagues that they should be submitting requests now for items that will need to be distributed in X amount of time.

5. Some departments will have a clear priority over others. For instance, fund-raising often has a high priority. If they suddenly need an e-mail or website promotion, their needs will push everyone else's projects out of the way.

   • Determine who has that priority and make it clear to everyone and why it is so. By being transparent, you can nip frustration in the bud.

   • Prioritizing fund-raising over others is easy, since this area brings money in. The conversations will be more difficult if you are pitting two otherwise similar areas against each other (e.g., children vs. adults programming).

## TIPS

Remember to schedule out your monthly repetitive tasks in advance. It may work for you to block this time out a year in advance. Then set yourself an assignment in eleven months to block out the time for the next year. You may be able to automatically schedule these tasks through your preferred calendar software.

I recommend colleagues send you marketing requests with a minimum due date of 6 to 8 weeks before the distribution date a publicity item (e.g. flyer) needs to go out. This way you have time to react to unexpected tasks, meetings, and due dates. Note this on your ingest form if you use one (Guide 7: "Ingest Form Setup").

Once you set your submission deadline in-house, it will be difficult to move it further back. If in doubt, add a longer time from the date of submission to the first distribution day.

Some places require events to be planned six months in advance. Others have no set guidelines. Your job will be to introduce this concept to your colleagues. Expect a bit of pushback.

Whatever your submission deadline is, you will notice that your calendar will neatly fill up that many weeks ahead. If you are available for non-regular items like user-requested training sessions (e.g., one-on-one help sessions), you may find it difficult to meet those requests in a timely manner. Those "free hours" you set aside each week will come in handy for these requests.

### Resources
• Cecily Walker, in episode 99 of *Circulating Ideas*, recommends watching "Project Management Foundations: Small Projects" to help you learn the documentation and paperwork aspects of project management.[1]

**WATCH OUT!**
Some deadlines will need to be strictly met, especially for outside groups. If a press release has to be in on Thursday by noon, you cannot send out "just one more" on Friday. You have already missed the deadline. If that happens, talk with your colleagues again and remind them that the deadlines are firm.

Consider being vague about when those hard deadlines are to your colleagues. If they know that you actually have until noon on Thursdays, they may try to send you a press release at 11:55 a.m. This may be after you already e-mailed your contact for the week. At the latest, ask for the press release to be submitted to you the day before it is scheduled for distribution.

## GUIDE 9: Understand Your Needs

**YOUR GOAL**
There are many ways to handle project management (PM). Before you get overwhelmed with all the endless tasks coming your way, you should set aside time to think about what you need to do. You can then decide on how to set up your PM system.

**DIFFICULTY LEVEL** Hard.

**TIME** Three hours.

**COST** Free in most cases.

**WHAT YOU NEED TO START**
You should know the scope of your job, so that you know what to track (Guide 2: "Outline Your Job Scope"). It is also helpful to start this with a project in mind that includes a few tasks, so you can see what it is like to enter it in your new PM setup.

**TOOLS**
- If you are going digital in your project management system, consider Asana, Basecamp ($), Google Calendar, or Trello.
- If you are going print or analog, consider a calendar, corkboards, note cards, notebooks, and sticky notes.

**WHAT YOU NEED TO KNOW**
You will likely mix and match various options to come up with your perfect PM system. No single tool can do everything that works for your needs.

A *project* refers to a single marketing push you are working on (e.g., summer reading). Project management is how you keep track of all the things you need to complete your work. With a strong PM system in place, you can rely on your past work and not worry about forgetting anything that needs to be done today or next month. In order to achieve this nirvana, you need to be diligent and stick to and update your system as new items come in.

**STEPS**

1. Brainstorm how you are going to organize your tasks. Mine are organized by whether they are small one-off tasks, year-round projects that repeat each month, or if they need to be shared with others. My work areas are organized like this:

    a. Inbox: This is a catch-all for all projects that come in.

    b. E-Mails and Social Media: This produces a calendar feed which is shared with colleagues (using Asana).

    c. Book Groups: This is a year-round intensive marketing plan with monthly repeating tasks.

2. For your Inbox, you need to know how you are going to gather publicity requests (Guide 5: "How to Gather Marketing Requests"). Consider how you will get those requests into your Inbox.

    • In Asana, you can forward e-mails to an address and have them added to your Inbox automatically.

3. Think about:

    a. How do you think and visualize your work?

    b. Do you like calendars, checklists, spreadsheets?

    c. How sortable, searchable, and filterable is the solution you are looking at?

4. Next read through each guide in this chapter to narrow in on your preferred PM system.

**TIPS**

Once you are familiar with your system, you should be able to add big projects within twenty minutes. To see how I use my project management setup, see Guide 17: "Example of a Complete Marketing Workflow."

**WATCH OUT!**

It is tempting to spend a long time working out the perfect project management system. Don't fall into this trap. You can always make adjustments over time as you come to understand your work and your own preferences better.

## GUIDE 10: Desired Capabilities

### DESIRED CAPABILITIES OF A PROJECT MANAGEMENT SYSTEM

How you think about tracking your projects is unique to you. Fortunately, most of us think in ways which are shared by other people. If you pick a PM system that matches the way you think, your life will be easier. For example, I am a visual person who likes lists, so a system that includes visuals and lists is key to help me reach my productivity goals.

### CALENDAR VIEWS

What is going on this month? This week? Today? If you choose a system that allows you to look at a calendar view, this is a familiar display that others can understand when you show them how long it will take to work on their project (especially if they are visual thinkers). A familiar calendar format is less intimidating than Gantt charts (see below). Figure 4.1 is an example from Asana.

**FIGURE 4.1**
**Screenshot of Asana.com's calendar view display**

### GANTT CHARTS

For diehard project managers, only a Gantt chart (see figure 4.2) can help them track a project over time. A Gantt chart is a time line with blocks that show at what time points the different aspects of a project will be happening.

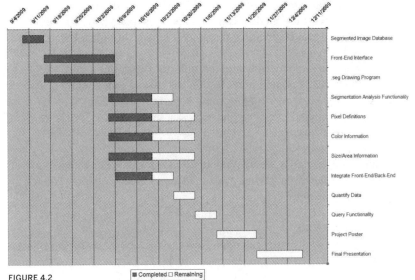

FIGURE 4.2
**Sample Gantt chart**

## KANBAN

You should use this method if you like to visualize tasks as cards that can be moved between columns as they go through their life cycle. Trello (https://trello .com) is built around the kanban method (see figure 4.3). Each column name can be customized to a stage in the project's development (e.g., To Do, Work in Progress, Finished, Cancelled). Then each card contains a single task or project that needs to be completed. As the item moves from one column to another, you can easily see how many projects are in progress, or even if a project has stalled out at some point. In Trello, clicking on a card allows you to add checklists, attachments, due dates, and assign the card to someone. Sticky notes or index cards on a wall can be used for an analog version of this.

FIGURE 4.3
**Screenshot of Trello.com's kanban display**

## TASKS AND SUBTASKS

When you have a new project, you will want to break it down into tasks and subtasks. Tasks are the main items you need to do for that project (e.g., create a flyer). A task is broken down into smaller components, or subtasks, which need to be done before that item can be completed (e.g., get a headshot for a flyer, print the flyer, distribute the flyer).

Depending on your system, you may be able to assign due dates, the person responsible for that task, and add notes to the task. Asana.com is built around this entire concept. As you complete a task or subtask, you can then check it off. To see an example of a project broken into tasks and subtasks, see Guide 15: "Publicity Plans."

## ASSIGN DATES

To get the most out of your system, you should assign due dates to each task and subtask. Some systems will then send you e-mail alerts to let you know when a task is coming up or is past due.

## ASSIGN A DATE RANGE

A feature that works well with calendar views is the ability to set a project or task to span a date range. That range is most likely the start and end dates of the project. You could use this to keep track of different displays in your building, for example. Then, by opening up calendar view, you can easily see which displays are visible all over the building during a specific time frame. Are there any common-alities between these displays? Can you promote more than one at a time? A date range view makes these patterns easier to discover.

## ASSIGN PEOPLE

If you are working with more than one person on a project or task, you could add them to your system and assign them portions of the work. If you are managing a small team, this would be an excellent addition. You could then see at a glance where everyone is on the project. Most online systems allow you to set up noti-fications to be sent out when tasks are assigned to a person, and when a task is completed or is past due.

## PROJECT TEMPLATES

Many of your tasks will be recurring ones. If your software allows you to create project templates, your work will be even more efficient. An example of this is that you have a monthly campaign which has ten tasks that need to be completed each month. At the end of the month, you could create a new task with subtasks that are identical to the month you just finished. This work is not difficult, but it does take up your valuable time. An ideal system would allow you to create that monthly campaign, add all the tasks, and then save it as a template which can be used over and over again. The only thing you need to do then is to add due dates.

## GUIDE 11: Analog vs. Digital

The great thing about project management systems (or tools) is that you can choose to go old school with paper, or you can go all-digital. The best system is the one that works for you. Figure 4.4 offers a comparison. Your perfect system may not match how someone else manages their information.

|  | Pros | Cons |
|---|---|---|
| **Analog** | • Free<br>• 100% customizable<br>• Can expand on a wall to see all aspects at once | • Difficult to share revisions<br>• Harder to share<br>• May not have backups<br>• Easier to lose<br>• Need a printer to add printouts |
| **Digital** | • Easy to share<br>• Easy to update<br>• Setup notifications<br>• Often can access from the cloud anywhere | • Cannot see all aspects at once<br>• May cost money<br>• Customer support may be lacking<br>• Limited to features of the system |

FIGURE 4.4
**Table comparing analog and digital project management tools**

## GUIDE 12: Comparison of Project Management Tools

Each of the systems below offers ways to help you keep track of everything you need to do in your work. However, no single product can do everything, so you will likely mix and match various products to come up with a system that works for you. There are many PM tools to choose from. The tools shown in figure 4.5 have free accounts, which in some cases can be upgraded for additional features. (Basecamp.com is also popular, but offers no free option.) The last column in the figure is how these tools help me.

| | Pros | Cons | My Use |
|---|---|---|---|
| **Airtable** | • Multiple views like calendar, spreadsheet, and kanban<br>• Most capabilities of a spreadsheet<br>• Attach images and checklists<br>• Very flexible use<br>• Embed into other websites | • Limited records (e.g. items) for free users<br>• Display of individual record items is less attractive than other solutions<br>• Documentation is not always clear | • Could use as a customer relations manager (CRM)<br>• Track marketing assets |
| **Asana** | • Offers task lists and subtasks<br>• Assign tasks and add due dates<br>• Attach images and write comments<br>• Create multiple project areas<br>• Can check off tasks<br>• Can duplicate tasks<br>• Nice printouts<br>• Calendar view<br>• Offers a calendar feed for other programs<br>• Great for team project management<br>• Archive projects<br>• Reorder tasks by drag and drop | • Requires mobile app to use on your phone<br>• Duplicated tasks require some cleanup<br>• Paid version is expensive<br>• Templates are a paid feature<br>• Start and end dates for a task are a paid feature<br>• Cannot edit printouts before printing<br>• Great documentation, but is overwhelming<br>• Additional click required to search completed tasks | • Tracks everything I need to do<br>• Single place to store information<br>• Copy communications into it |

| | | | |
|---|---|---|---|
| **Google Calendar** | • Calendar views: day, week, month<br>• Create recurring time blocks with ease (e.g., social media)<br>• Visually see how time is assigned<br>• Easy to share<br>• Add location information<br>• Add comments<br>• Helps schedule meetings<br>• Show/hide availability<br>• Export data | • Cannot add attachments to events<br>• Search is not strong<br>• No checklists<br>• Exported data is not very attractive | • Block out time for each project<br>• Compare my calendar against desk shift calendars |
| **Google Sheets** | • Sharable spreadsheet<br>• Works a lot like Excel<br>• Add-ons are available for new features<br>• Export in multiple formats<br>• Anywhere access | • Inserted images need to be manually resized<br>• Inserted images cannot be "locked" to a cell<br>• Little control over printed layout<br>• Importing data from another cell can be slow | • Use for personal knowledge base<br>• Track statistics due to share-ability |
| **Trello** | • Kanban layout<br>• Columns can be renamed<br>• Cards (i.e., projects) are easy to create<br>• Attach items to cards<br>• Assign cards and add due dates<br>• Integrated access to Google services<br>• Create multiple kanban boards<br>• Add checklists to cards<br>• Drag cards between columns<br>• Archive cards<br>• Usable app | • Power-Ups (additional features) allotments are based on a tiered price range<br>• Obscures other cards when working on one | • A board for marketing inbox<br>• A board for social media tracking<br>• Use for both personal and work |

FIGURE 4.5
**Table comparing different project management tools**

# GUIDE 13: Personal Knowledge Base

You do so many different things as part of your work. If you were unable to come to work tomorrow, would someone else be able to step in and carry on? A personal knowledge base (PKB) helps you know exactly where to look for information to do your job when you need it.

By setting up a PKB, you can keep track of design specs, lists of outside contacts, tutorials, and anything else that you may need to revisit again later. The most important thing is to use the PKB consistently, update it, and later share it with your successor and any other colleagues. Depending on your technology comfort skills, you can use a wide variety of tools to set up your PKB.

## KNOWLEDGE TO CAPTURE
- Design specifications
- Style and branding guidelines (Guide 3: "Know Your Branding")
- Tutorials
- Locations of where you save your work (Guide 18: "File Management")
- List of public relations contacts (Guide 59: "Document Your Public Relations Contacts")
- When to contact media outlets (Chapter 9: "Outside Contacts")
- Where to find stock photos (Guide 24: "Images")
- Log-in information for accounts
- List of marketing offerings (Guide 4: "Make an Inventory of Market Offerings")
- List of acronyms you use

## EASY OPTIONS
Evernote (https://evernote.com) offers a downloadable program for off-line access, a web interface, and a browser extension to make it easy to share and save web pages. It can come free or paid.

Spreadsheets (Excel and Google Drive) are easy to create and share. However, they can be hard to read for longer text. They can come free or paid.

Trello (https://trello.com/) captures information on cards that are organized into columns. Each card can be edited to include text, images, and due dates, and can be assigned to colleagues. The interface is drag and drop. Trello can come free or paid.

## ADVANCED OPTIONS
MediaWiki (https://www.mediawiki.org/wiki/MediaWiki) was originally used for Wikipedia. It is very difficult to set up and use. If your organization has an intranet wiki setup already, use that first. MediaWiki is free.

TiddlyWiki (https://tiddlywiki.com) is a self-contained wiki that exists in one HTML file. It is easy to back up, customize, and use, but it does take a little time to learn the system. Your TiddlyWiki should be accessible years from now, since it relies on no company's infrastructure to support it. It is free.

## GUIDE 14: Internal Tracking System

**YOUR GOAL**
How do you keep track of decisions you've made and how your efforts are going from year to year? An internal tracking system (ITS) will ensure that you know how you're doing.

**DIFFICULTY LEVEL** Easy.

**TIME** Fifteen minutes.

**COST** Free.

**WHAT YOU NEED TO START**
Decide how you want to record the information you need to track over the long term. Do you prefer a digital solution, or paper?

**TOOLS**
   • Spreadsheet or grid paper

**WHAT YOU NEED TO KNOW**
The internal tracking system can be built into the personal knowledge base (Guide 13: "Personal Knowledge Base") or into your project management system (Chapter 4: "Set Up Project Management"). The purpose of an ITS is twofold: to help you keep track of decisions and to monitor your stats over the long term. Any of the software that I have mentioned for a personal knowledge base or project management system may also be used for an ITS. Spreadsheets are my preferred method, since they are free as well as easy to understand.

**STEPS**

*Tracking Decisions*
It can be difficult to remember why you shut down a social media account or no longer send press releases to certain outlets (Guide 62: "Press Releases"). The ITS helps you quickly justify past decisions if questions arise as to why you are no longer doing something or you started something new.

1. Open up your spreadsheet software of choice and name the file.
2. Across the top row, add these columns:
   a. Date: When the decision was made
   b. Item: What the decision was about
   c. Outcome: What the decision or change is
   d. Responsibility: Who made the decision
   e. Why: Explain the reasoning for the decision

3. Start a new row for each item you add to your spreadsheet.

4. Write short descriptions for the item and outcome columns.

### Long-Term Stats

At the end of every major campaign, you have been collecting stats about how well the campaign did. When it's time for that campaign to resume for a new year, it's helpful to look back and use the previous years as a benchmark to see how you did this year. Those previous stats can also help you decide on any changes to make to your marketing. The example below shows how to set up a spreadsheet for a Spring Fundraiser from year to year. The setup of this long-term stats spreadsheet only takes a few minutes, but it can take an hour or more to input each year's data as you check on each stat.

1. Make sure you collect stats at the end of each major campaign (e.g., attendance, page hits, e-mail opens and clicks, social media engagement).

2. Create a spreadsheet for each major campaign (e.g., Spring Fundraiser).

3. The fields will differ depending upon what you are tracking. For the Spring Fundraiser, I use these columns:

   a. Type: Broad categories of e-mail, paid ad, print, social media, website, e-mail

   b. Kind: What the publicity piece specifically was (e.g., which newspaper name, Twitter, website Call to Action, Single Event e-mail)

   c. Date: This can be a single date or a range (e.g., a paid ad).

   d. Opens: This is applicable only to e-mails.

   e. Clicks/Engagements: This is a combined column for e-mail clicks and social media post interactions.

   f. Visitors: This is for website pages.

   g. Impressions: How many people saw or how many times a post was viewed for social media accounts. Each platform may count these numbers differently.

   h. Notes: This may be a link to the social media post, a short explanation, or an analysis.

   i. Recommendation: Any thoughts on how to do better next year.

| Year | Attendees | Diff to PY | Website Page Views | Diff to PY | Website Unique Views | Diff to PY |
|------|-----------|-----------|--------------------|-----------|----------------------|-----------|
| 2019 | 329 | 15.3% | 3485 | 139.6% | 3209 | 140% |
| 2018 | 189 | -32.7% | 1454 | -28.2% | 1337 | -26.7% |
| 2017 | 281 | | 2026 | | 1823 | |

FIGURE 4.6
**Table of a long-term campaign created**

4. After the data has been entered, add a totals row.

5. Save this first sheet as *Template.*

6. Make a copy of the template sheet and then rename it to the year of the campaign.

7. On each year's sheet, I add other mini-tables to surround the main data collection. They may be:

    a. Overall summary

    b. Interesting discoveries

    c. Down areas

    d. Quick comparison charts from previous years

8. The final sheet is titled *Comparisons.* For the Spring Fundraiser, these are the column headers:

    a. Year

    b. Attendees: How many attended

    c. Difference to Prior Year: This is written as a percentage.

    d. Website Page Views

    e. Diff to PY: This is shorthand for item c. It refers to the numbers in d.

    f. E-Mail Opens

    g. Diff to PY

    h. Clicks/Engagements

    i. Diff to PY

    j. Notes

9. After entering all your data for the year, make sure to then add the highlights to your *Comparison* sheet. See figure 4.6 for an example of the *Comparison* spreadsheet.

## TIPS

When working on a spreadsheet, consider color-coding it in order to highlight outstanding positive numbers or low ones. I use green and red but beware of red-green color blindness for other users (Guide 21: "Design").

Try to use your spreadsheet's formulas to add up your numbers. This way, if you make a change later, the total will update to the new value.

| Email Opens | Diff to PY | Clicks or Engagements | Diff to PY | Notes |
|---|---|---|---|---|
| 1125 | 26.1% | 821 | 60% | New author with journalism background |
| 8930 | -8.3% | 513 | 19.9% | New author |
| 9734 | | 428 | | Established popular author |

It takes a little work to figure it out, but try to reference the data in other sheets by using the formulas in Excel or Google Sheets.[2]

**WATCH OUT!**
Since decision and long-term stat tracking sheets will be passed to your successor, keep your comments on them professional.

## GUIDE 15: Publicity Plans

**YOUR GOAL**
You can impress your colleagues by presenting to them a publicity plan for their project.

**DIFFICULTY LEVEL** Easy.

**TIME** Thirty minutes.

**COST** Free.

**WHAT YOU NEED TO START**
Your colleagues need to supply you with information about their project. Ideally, they should have submitted their request through your preferred request system of e-mail (Guide 6: "E-Mail System Setup") or ingest form (Guide 7: "Ingest Form Setup").

**TOOLS**
- Your project management software
- Word processor

**WHAT YOU NEED TO KNOW**
This guide assumes that you are familiar with what marketing items you can offer, which will speed up the development of the publicity plan (Guide 4: "Make an Inventory of Marketing Offerings"). It is also helpful if you know information about your social media (Guide 71: "Social Media Tips") and e-mail newsletter audiences (Guide 27: "E-Mail Newsletters"). You should have a rough idea of how long it takes for the various marketing items to be created.

**STEPS**
1. Look over the request submitted by your colleagues. If the information is complete and includes information about the audience, the time line, and suggested publicity venues, proceed.
   - If not, ask for more information.

| | |
|---|---|
| ☐ Amanda: Signs for Rainy Day Cart | due June 5 |
| Susie Skerrett created the Rainy Day movie cart at Darien Library. | |
| The signs would fill the side of either end of the cart. | |
| ☑ Amanda: ~~Meet with Susie to discuss her signage ideas.~~ | due April 10 |
| ☑ Amanda: ~~Create a publicity plan.~~ | due April 10 |
| ☐ Amanda: Measure cart's sides. | due April 17 |
| ☐ Amanda: Draft a design and share it for feedback. | due April 17 |
| ☐ Amanda: Make adjustments. | due May 1 |
| ☐ Amanda: Print a test copy out to check the fitting. | due May 2 |
| ☐ Amanda: Make adjustments to fit. | due May 21 |
| ☐ Amanda: Send final designs to printer for placement on foam board. | due May 23 |
| ☐ Amanda: Attach signs to cart. | |

Amanda
She's interested in changing the language from RAINY to WEATHER . Ask her for details.

FIGURE 4.7
**Print preview screenshot of a publicity plan created in Asana.com**

2. Depending on your project management tool, the request may already be in your system with each requested item already listed as a to-do item. Or you may need to set it up yourself by creating a task for each marketing item.

3. Do you agree with your colleagues' suggested marketing/outreach items?
   • If not, contact them to make suggestions and explain why.

4. Now that the request is in your project management system, look at the day the first publicity piece needs to go out. Work backwards to assign due dates for each item. You will do this in conjunction with your calendar as you block out the time needed to create the item.

5. Once you are done, print out a copy of your publicity plan and present it to them. (See figure 4.7.)

**TIPS**
Publicity plans offer a wow factor. If colleagues are not used to seeing their tasks broken out with dates, your plan will look very professional. You are showing them that you're serious about marketing their project. Staff may then do you the courtesy of pinning the plan to their wall. This has a positive impact on your reputation whenever your colleagues refer to it with other staff.

You should overestimate the creation time for each item (Guide 8: "Time Management"). You never know when an interruption, illness, learning curve, or lack of inspiration may occur.

Try to get the final item finished a week before the first date the item is needed to go out. This gives you padding in case of a dire time crunch.

Use a highlighter to mark pivotal dates.

**WATCH OUT!**

If you have to rely on others to complete aspects of the publicity plan, you may end up with blank due-date spots. When you hand the plan over, give a brief explanation as to why the date is blank.

## GUIDE 16: Marketing Strategy

**YOUR GOAL**

You can tackle projects as they come up day to day, but how do you plan for the long term?

**DIFFICULTY LEVEL** Hard.

**TIME** Four hours.

**COST** Free.

**WHAT YOU NEED TO START**

You should have the desire and the time to think strategically over the long term. It is advised that you have in-depth familiarity with the marketing efforts your organization has done, who your target audiences are, and your organization's strategic plan. You should have completed an inventory of your marketing offerings (Guide 4: "Make an Inventory of Marketing Offerings").

**TOOLS**

- Internet access
- Word processor

**WHAT YOU NEED TO KNOW**

Trying to go into the full details of developing a marketing strategy is beyond the scope of this book. This guide points to some resources that can help you figure out your long-term planning. Please note that the language used to describe this document may differ across organizations (e.g., marketing plan, marketing strategy).

The point of a marketing strategy is to help you plan how you will improve your work and outreach over a set time period. While the strategy should have specific goals that you would like to achieve (e.g., increased attendance), it should not include detailed implementation plans. The marketing strategy guides you in how to use your time and where to focus your attention and energy during the time period.

**STEPS**

1. Set aside time to focus on developing a marketing strategy. You will want time to:

   • Research other organizations' strategies.
   • Review your organization's vision, mission, and operational and strategic plans.
   • Note the goals your organization wants to achieve during the upcoming time period.
   • Examine the targeted audiences you wish to reach and their desires, needs, and goals.
   • Discover what major activities and initiatives individual departments will be working on.
   • Schedule yourself time to work on this project; sharing it, writing revisions of it, and then implementing it.

2. Review the marketing strategy plans from nonprofits and for-profits alike.

   a. What are some great ideas that would work for you?
   b. Is there something you would like to try?

3. Use the strategic plans you looked at in step 2 or use templates to help plan your document.

4. It is important to include an assessment or evaluation mechanism within your marketing strategy. If you don't set real-number goals for yourself, you won't know if you met your objectives.

5. Discuss your marketing strategic plan with your supervisor so they can sign off on your plan. In some organizations, your supervisor may need permission from someone above them before your plan can be put into action since it impacts the entire organization.

6. Once your strategic plan has been approved, set aside time to work on implementing it. This may involve creating spreadsheets to track your goals, quarterly assessments to write a summary of your work, and scheduling meetings to get other staff on board.

*Resources*

   • South Central Library System, "Implementing a Library Marketing Plan," https://web.archive.org/web/20180501050235/http://www.scls.info/pr/toolkit/marketing_plan/implementation
   • New Mexico State Library, "Library Marketing Plan Workbook," www.nmstatelibrary.org/docs/development/planning/Marketing_Plan_Workbook.pdf
   • Toronto Public Library, "Program Marketing Plan," https://drive.google.com/drive/folders/0B3YB1OvhBWucODFjYmU4MzUtZDI5OS00YjA1L WE3Y2MtM2YzNjgzMjY3OTcy?ddrp=1&hl=en

- How to Market @ your library™: "Creating Your Five-Year Campaign Participant Manual," http://multimedia.3m.com/mws/media/971860/ creating-5-year-campaign-wonewok-participant-manual.pdf
- Columbus Metro Library, "Marketing Plan Strategy," https://docs.google .com/document/d/18K17XTZzSD9NFgz_9tZnJT9K06ZO1pUwg7wibRY en1E/edit
- Lac La Biche County Libraries, "Library Marketing Plan 2016–2020," http:// files.townlife.com/public/uploads/documents/18737/Library_Marketing _Plan_2016-2020.pdf
- Smithsonian Institution, Office of Policy and Analysis, "Audience Building: Marketing Art Museums," https://www.si.edu/Content/opanda/docs/ Rpts2001/01.10.MarketingArt.Final.pdf
- Museums and Galleries of New South Wales, "Marketing for Museums," https://mgnsw.org.au/sector/resources/online-resources/organisation -management/marketing-museums-factsheet

The Toronto and Columbus libraries' plans were found in *Library Journal* in Alison Circle's article, "Marketing Plan Templates."[3]

## TIPS

You may not need a complex, detailed plan. Develop what you have the resources and time to work on.

Sometimes your assessment cannot be shown in numbers (e.g., increased ticket purchases), but in stories of impact. A great end-of-year report of your work would include a mixture of both types of assessment.

If you cannot get approval to create a formal marketing strategy, set yourself some goals to work towards on your own. This will help you communicate the value of your work at your annual review.

Formulate an elevator speech to explain the importance of using a long-term strategy to shape your day-to-day work. For example, if your goal is to get mentioned on the local news more often, you may need to expend less energy on posting on social media during this period. When questioned, you want to speak with authority and knowledge about decisions like this. A written plan will help back you up.

## WATCH OUT!

Beware of feeling overwhelmed when you find marketing plans that are dozens of pages long. You are not in competition with those organizations. You should only do what works for your organization's needs.

Stay flexible. Just because you set a goal for the year doesn't mean that you will be able to implement it. This can be frustrating, but you are part of a larger organization whose needs are fluid.

## GUIDE 17: Example of a Complete Marketing Workflow

**YOUR GOAL**

Now that we've gone over each separate piece in setting up a project management system, how do you integrate them into one workflow? This guide presents my personal workflow using free tools.

**DIFFICULTY LEVEL** Intermediate.

**TIME** Twenty minutes.

**COST** Free.

**WHAT YOU NEED TO START**

To replicate this system, you need to know what your marketing offerings are (Guide 4: Make an Inventory of Marketing Offerings"), have a system for gathering marketing requests (Guide 5: "How to Gather Marketing Requests"), and have set up your own project management system (Chapter 4: "Set Up Project Management").

**TOOLS**

- Asana.com
- E-mail
- Google Calendar
- JotForm.com

**WHAT YOU NEED TO KNOW**

This guide applies to a bigger campaign, not just someone wanting a single social media post. The campaign includes multiple publicity pieces that need to be tracked. The time estimate is for how long I need to take the average submitted request and get it filed within my project management system.

The backbone of my system is Asana.com. It allows you to create "big picture" projects which contains tasks. Each task is actually a single campaign or project I am working on. Tasks usually have subtasks for what needs to happen to complete that campaign/project.

My "big picture" project boards are:

- Inbox: This is for all campaigns that do not go into the other project boards.
- Press Releases: Each task is for a single week, with subtasks of items that need to go out.
- E-Mails and Social Media: This tracks e-mail newsletters, tweets, and Facebook posts.
- Book Groups Monthly Plan: This is an intense, monthly recurring task that is big enough to get its own board.

**STEPS**

1. A colleague submits a marketing request via the JotForm ingest form at least six weeks before the first piece needs to go out.
   - If the project is something big, such as Summer Reading, or they will need to send items out to a professional designer or printer, the staff send in their requests at least three months in advance.

2. JotForm notifies me of the submitted ingest form via e-mail. I look the form over to see if I have any questions about the request. If so, I reply back. I will later manually copy over my colleagues' response or summarize it in the Asana task.

3. I forward the e-mail to the project e-mail address given to me via Asana.[4] The project board that the e-mail goes to is titled *Inbox*.

4. Once a request is in *Inbox*, I add subtasks for each marketing piece that needs to be done. I also create subtasks for when I need to remind people to send me information.

5. In Google Calendar, I block out time slots for each subtask (e.g., make a flyer, e-mail a staff reminder, and send to printer).

6. As each subtask is scheduled in Google Calendar, I switch back to Asana to put in that date. The subtask whose date happens first is then assigned to the entire task. This way when I look over my master list of tasks in *Inbox* each week, I can see which task has a subtask that is due soon.

7. Each subtask is assigned to myself or others within Asana.

8. Once the request has been completely scheduled out, I print out the task as a publicity plan and give it to the requester (Guide 15: "Publicity Plans").

9. While working through the request's items, I return to Asana to check each subtask item off. Then I change the task's due date to the next due date.

10. Images are attached to the task, and communications with the staff and notes are added as comments. Any final comments, reviews, or reports are copied in as a comment.

11. When each subtask has been completed, the task is finally checked off. Asana archives the task to hide it from view.

**TIPS**

The last subtask is usually after the event has passed. This is a reminder to go collect stats on how many attended, social media information, website visits to the page, and so on.

While not every request is a major task with subtasks, every item that needs to get done is entered into the *Inbox* or into a specific project board. That way, no request is missed. I also have a complete history of my work which can be pulled up.

It is important to assign dates to tasks as they come in so they are entered into the time tracking system in Google Calendar. This is the secret to nothing being forgotten. Then each day can be approached with confidence that you are on-task.

In *Inbox,* create a task titled *Ideas:* with the colon. This task will act as a header to put other tasks underneath it. You can do this with anything but capturing your ideas for future projects within your *Inbox* will help you find things to do when you have a spare moment.

If possible, try to get others to use Asana with you. Then you can assign tasks and subtasks directly to them. They can also add notes and answer your questions there without you needing to copy their responses in from e-mail. If no one is interested, that is fine too.

The most time-consuming part of this workflow—aside from creating the publicity items—is adding all the dates to each subtask.

## WATCH OUT!

Try not to get too caught up when task due dates turn red as the date passes. I use a project titled *E-Mails and Social Media* to schedule out all e-mail newsletters and most social media posts. Each item is added as a task, with the date it goes out as the assigned date. Only after the action has gone past do I check it off. If you were to look at a report of my Asana work, it would appear that I am late on completing most of my monthly assigned tasks. However, since we know what the reason is, that discrepancy can be explained.

## NOTES

1. Amanda L. Goodman and Michael Schofield, "Interview with Cecily Walker," August 16, 2016, *Circulating Ideas,* produced by Steve Thomas, podcast, https://circulatingideas.com/2016/08/16/episode-99-cecily-walker.

2. Microsoft, "Create or Change a Cell Reference," https://support.office.com/en-us/article/create-or-change-a-cell-reference-c7b8b95d-c594-4488-947e-c835903ce baa#bmcreate_a_cell_reference_to_another_wo; Andrew, "Reference Data from Other Sheets," https://support.google.com/docs/answer/75943.

3. Alison Circle, "Marketing Plan Templates," 2010, https://lj.libraryjournal.com/2010/02/opinion/bubble-room/marketing-plan-templates.

4. Asana, "Forward Emails to Turn Them into Asana Tasks," https://asana.com/guide/help/email/email-to-asana.

*chapter* 5

# Content Creation

THIS CHAPTER INTRODUCES YOU TO SOME IDEAS, CONCEPTS, AND TIPS related to the creation of marketing content. The guides in this chapter will not show you how to create these types of content. The tools, techniques, trends, and best practices to create content will evolve from where they are today. Some areas are explored with a greater level of detail in their own separate guides.

## GUIDE 18: File Management

Everyone in your organization should use good file management practices. This will increase productivity and efficiency. However, not everyone is ready to make the leap. You and your team can be the trailblazers. If you set up a file management system and then follow it and enforce its use consistently, you will not lose another file. What is even better is that you can customize this system to match how you think.

### FILE-NAMING SYSTEM

First, start writing file names that are descriptive. For example, use the name *2019_ summer_reading_plan.docx* instead of *plan.docx*. By including more keywords in the title, you will be able to use your computer's search system to help you locate a file if you save it somewhere unexpected. However, don't go overboard. Use as few words as possible while still maintaining a quick understanding of what the file contains. If you decide to use abbreviations, include a key somewhere (maybe in a simple text file in the topmost-level folder) which shows that *SR* stands for *Summer Reading*.

If you or your colleagues will be managing a website, insist on using good file-naming techniques for all uploads (videos, documents, images). If everyone uses the same system, this makes it easier to read and find files later on.

- Leave no spaces between words; instead, use hyphens or underscores.
- Use all-lowercase letters, or practice camel case; for example, SummerReadingPlan.
- Select a consistent naming system and enforce it.

Why follow these rules? Because modern computer systems can generally handle our human input methods, but other humans may have trouble reading them or typing them. For example, if you have spaces in your file names, the file extension will look more like *2019%20summer%20reading%20plan.pdf*, which is much harder to read and slower to type than *2019_summer_reading_plan.pdf*. This is also a best practice in many other disciplines.

### Versioning

When you are figuring out the design or text for a project, save a copy of each version. You never know when you will decide that the third design was your favorite. Differentiate between each version with a two-digit number at the end of the file name. For example, use *2019–04_blog_header_01.jpg*. Use the leading zero so that if you make more than nine versions, the file names will remain in order when you sort them.

You may name the version you settle on *2019–04_blog_header_final.jpg*. A better practice is to create a folder and throw all the rejected versions in there so you don't confuse them with the final version. Save those attempts for later as sources of inspiration or for blog posts about your creation process.

### Dates

If you are making content that should be easily accessible by date, add the date to the front of the file name. That way, when you sort by date, your files will be in the correct order. Use this standard: YYYY-MM-DD, as set by the International Organization for Standardization (ISO). This particular order is ISO 8601.[1] Your file name would then look like *2019–04–28_amelia_earhart_diary.docx*. You may also leave out the dashes between the numbers but keep that underscore between the date and the text. Whichever method you select, use it consistently.

### Resources

- Stanford Libraries,"Best Practices for File Naming," https://library.stanford .edu/research/data-management-services/data-best-practices/best-practices -file-naming
- Williams College Special Collections, "File-Naming Tutorial," https:// specialcollections.williams.edu/recordsmanagement/file-naming-tutorial

## FOLDER SYSTEM

Of equal importance to file-naming systems, you also want to set up a well-organized folder system. How this system is structured depends on your own particular tastes. Some suggested options are to file by year, department, recurring program type (e.g., book sale), or format (printing, digital, social media, web, video). You can also mix these organization types as you see fit. Just put folders within each of these top levels to cover for specific projects.

My system looks like this:

- Digital Signs
- Printing
    - 2017
    - 2018
        - Book Sale
            - Summer Book Sale
            - Winter Book Sale
    - 2019
- Social Media

Notice that these folders do not follow the no spaces and lowercase rules. Since these items are stored on a hard drive and not online, I felt confident in naming the folders in this way.

## TEMPLATES

I recommend keeping the original design documents for everything you create. This means saving not only the final PDF, but also the InDesign, Photoshop, or Word file that you created the design in. If, for example, the printed sign gets damaged or you made a typo, you can quickly produce a new copy. In the same folder, keep all the assets that went into making the piece (usually artwork or a copy of a special font).

For many marketing pieces, you will have opportunities to reuse them down the road. Some programs happen every year, so you can quickly pull something together within minutes. It will likely take you about a year to get most of these templates made. But just think about how much faster your work will be next year! To make a new copy, just open the original creation file and then save a new copy of it.

## MAKE BACKUPS

Since you are going through all this hard work, make sure that everything is safely backed up. Check with your IT department for internal options. Otherwise, depending on your organization's security policies, you can back up to a service like Google Drive or Dropbox. Another local option is to have an additional external hard drive to copy your files to on a regular basis. This option is the weakest in most instances. If you had manually backed up two weeks ago and today your computer crashed, you will lose everything you did in the last two weeks.

## GUIDE 19: Content

### SETTING UP YOUR FILE SYSTEM

Check out file management in Guide 18: "File Management" for advice on file naming, versioning, dates, folder, templates, and backups for your files. The most important idea is to keep everything you create that you spend more than two minutes on. You can then work from it again in the future without starting from scratch.

### CONTENT TYPES

You can create most of the items that you need to use in your work with access to a computer and a digital camera (i.e., the one in a smartphone). The types of content you can produce are in these categories: audio, e-mails, printed materials, social media, text, video, and web design. Your comfort level in making items in all of these formats may not be the same. Or you may be lucky enough to have staff who can handle the parts that you are not proficient in.

#### *Tools to Help You in Creation and/or Editing:*

- Adobe (https://www.adobe.com) is home to the most popular tools like Acrobat, InDesign, and Photoshop. It is paid.
- Atom (https://atom.io) is for text editing, web coding, and general writing. It is free.
- Audacity (https://www.audacityteam.org) is for recording or editing audio. It is free.
- Buffer (https://buffer.com) is for queuing up posts on various social media platforms. It can be free or paid.
- Canva (https://canva.com) is for image creation, especially for social media. It can be free or paid.
- Final Cut Pro (https://www.apple.com/final-cut-pro) is for advanced video editing. It is paid. Mac only.
- iMovie (https://www.apple.com/imovie) is for simple video editing. It is free. Mac only.
- Lightworks (https://www.lwks.com) is for video editing. It can be free or paid.
- Pixabay (https://pixabay.com) is for public-domain stock images. There are many sites like this one. It is free.
- Pixlr Editor (https://pixlr.com/editor) is for image editing. It is free.

### REUSABLE CONTENT

Your content can often be tweaked to work in a different context. For example, a book list can be turned into single social media posts in order to highlight each individual item. Or a quote from a video can be turned into a text quote image. For printed materials, you can reuse images from the poster to put on a bookmark. When it makes sense, try to squeeze the most you can out of each piece of content you create, and reuse it elsewhere.

**CUSTOMIZE PER THE AUDIENCE**

You can sometimes post the same video on different social media platforms, but the audiences may be different. If your Facebook page's followers are mostly women in their mid-forties, they may not be interested in the latest social media fad post you created for another platform's audience. If you have done the work of figuring out your audiences, you will have a better idea of where each piece of content should go (see Chapter 7: "Who Are Your Users?").

**CONTENT MARKETING**

When you are creating publicity materials, it is easy to keep thinking of your organization's goals. You hired a speaker to come in, so everyone should be interested in just the speaker's name and topic alone, right? No! People want to know *why* they should care and what is in it for them.

Sometimes your content may not be directly promoting any particular program or service. You may be looking to educate, inform, or entertain your users. Suppose, for example, you want to inform your users about which hard drives are the best for their computers. Backblaze, a data backup service, produces annual reports on its experiences on how different hard drive brands performed over the year.[2] This is useful information for anyone researching which hard drive is the most reliable one. Backblaze's reports are sometimes promoted on other sites like Lifehacker.[3] This sort of content marketing is invaluable for the company, but it can also be helpful for your users. Backblaze's agenda overall is to acquire more subscribers to its service, and it uses these helpful reports as a vehicle to deliver its promotional message.

Your organization can capitalize on social media by paying attention to what is trending and of interest on them. If you have special collections, you could share that you have medieval manuscripts if that is suddenly a hot topic of the day. You are not asking for donations or asking people directly to come in to your library, but you are raising interest in your collections. If all goes well, this may draw in more tangible benefits, but likely just getting word out about the cool stuff you offer might be the only immediate payout.

Check out Laura Solomon's book, *The Librarian's Nitty-Gritty Guide to Content Marketing*, for more details.

## GUIDE 20: Copyright

Each country has its own copyright laws governing the reproduction and financial rights owed to creators and publishers for the use of their work. For the purposes of this book, we will focus on American copyright law. Please note that I am not a lawyer. If you have any questions, seek legal counsel.

In general, anything that you create from the moment it is captured in a tangible format that can be shared (written, recorded, photographed, or drawn) is copyrighted automatically. Copyright law is complex.

*Resources*
- Full text of U.S. copyright law, https://www.copyright.gov/title17
- Berkman Center for Internet and Society, "Copyright for Librarians" course, http://cyber.harvard.edu/copyrightforlibrarians/Main_Page
- Berkman Center for Internet and Society, "Copyright for Librarians: The Essential Handbook," www.eifl.net/resources/copyright-librarians-essential-handbook
- Georgetown University Library, "Introduction to Copyright," https://www.library.georgetown.edu/copyright/introduction

## PUBLIC DOMAIN

Material that is in the "public domain" means that it is free for anyone to use, remix, and adapt to their own needs without attribution or payment to the original creator. Public domain can be granted through the expiration of copyright protection (the length varies in different countries) or if the creator voluntarily waives copyright. Remember that just because something goes into the public domain in one country doesn't mean it is within the public domain within your own country. Likewise, the first volume in a series of novels may go into the public domain, while the characters and stories in later books may still be under copyright.

The cheapest resource you can acquire is public domain items (audio, image, text, or video). Many websites claim to offer public domain items. Use your best judgment and read the website's terms. Do they seem trustworthy? If in doubt, go somewhere else. Keep in mind that it is easy to reproduce and distribute other people's copyrighted materials. But just because you found it on the Internet doesn't mean it is free for you to use.

## FAIR USE

The American fair use doctrine "promotes freedom of expression by permitting the unlicensed use of copyright-protected works in certain circumstances."[4] There are four considerations which judges use to evaluate whether the use of copyright material falls within fair use. These criteria are described by the U.S. Copyright Office:

1. The purpose and character of the use, including whether the use is of a commercial nature or is for nonprofit educational purposes
2. The nature of the copyrighted work
3. The amount and substantiality of the portion used in relation to the copyrighted work as a whole
4. The effect of the use upon the potential market for or value of the copyrighted work

Arguing that your use of copyrighted material counts as fair use is tricky and opens your organization up to be sued for copyright infringement. Working for a nonprofit or using material in a way that does not directly correlate to raising money does not fully cover your use of copyrighted material. Going to court to defend your use is expensive. In this author's opinion, it is best to avoid these gray waters and stick with purchasing rights, or use public domain and Creative Commons licensed works.

### CREATIVE COMMONS

Creative Commons (https://creativecommons.org) is a way to assist creators in allowing others to use their works within specified limitations. Creative Commons (CC) licenses can cover works that are audio, image, text, or video. There are a number of licenses available that grant you permission to use a work within the limits listed. A basic license will inform you:

1. May this work be used for commercial (i.e., money-making) purposes?
2. Do you need to always include the name of the creator wherever you use the work?
3. Is the link to where you found the work required?
4. Can you make modifications to the work (e.g., color changes, erasing, etc.)?
5. Do you need to include the name of the license and link back to it wherever you use the work?

Most CC licenses will require you, at a minimum, to write something similar to:

Photo by [name] / CC BY 2.0.

You would link *Photo* to the location you found the image. CC BY 2.0 would link to the license. You can use the Creative Commons search engine (https://search.creativecommons.org) to look for CC licensed works.

### WORKS FOR HIRE

Check your employment contract regarding who has the rights to "works for hire." There is likely a provision that states that anything you create as part of your job is copyrighted to your employer, not you. For your own portfolio, ask for permission to include your best pieces on your own website.

Additionally, if you hire a designer for a project, seek to purchase the exclusive rights for the design they create for your organization. This may come at an additional cost. If you choose this route, consider letting the designer continue to include the design in their portfolio to help them secure future work.

If you are purchasing a design from a website, you are often not buying exclusive rights to the use of that material. Others may also be able to purchase the same design and use it too.

## GUIDE 21: Design

The good news is that with today's web resources, you can make attractive content without a degree in graphic design or computer graphics. You should still have some knowledge of basic design principles (balance, color, repetition, size, layouts, fonts, texture), but a lot of the heavy lifting can be found through free or cheap templates that you can find online. Check your software for templates. Moreover, new mobile apps are always coming out to improve photos and videos taken with a smartphone.

### ACCESSIBLE CONTENT

You need to understand the challenges your users may have in accessing your content. Access usually means reading, seeing, or hearing for your marketing purposes. If you create interactive pieces that people can access digitally or in the real world (e.g., a scavenger hunt), how people would physically access the content becomes a concern.

#### Tips for Better Accessibility

*Large Fonts:* If your targeted audience is older, they may not be able to read smaller text fonts, so you should make sure that the most important information is big enough to be easily read. I recommend fonts no smaller than 16 points on print materials. If your material is going to be read from a distance, go even bigger.

*Avoid Jargon:* Use the language that your audience would use. Sometimes this involves you debating with a colleague about whether your audience would know what interlibrary loan means. When in doubt, try to use simple explanations like "Borrow books from other libraries."

*Color Blindness:* There are several different forms of color blindness, from being unable to distinguish between red and green to the rare complete lack of color perception. Color blindness affects more men than women. "As many as 8 percent of men and 0.5 percent of women with Northern European ancestry have the common form of red-green color blindness," says the National Eye Institute.[5] For your general purposes, avoid putting red text on a green background and vice versa.

*Captions:* Someone doesn't need to have complete hearing loss to benefit from captions. The person may not be familiar with the language being spoken, is in a noisy area, or has impaired hearing. Captions for videos are expensive and time-consuming to create, but if you can offer them, you should do so. This makes your content more accessible. For social media websites which auto-play videos, but not necessarily the audio, a user can still understand the video if captions are provided.

Your organization may be required by law to include captions. The University of California at Berkley stopped providing public access to its video lectures due to a lawsuit regarding accessibility that involved captions.[6]

## LAYOUTS

You should learn about grid systems. They will help you lay out all your print and digital content. A lot of layout design comes from just getting a feel for when things look off. Laying out a design may take you longer than completing the rest of the piece. However, it is the most important aspect of the piece. A design that is not well-balanced is not pleasing to look at. There is something to be said for breaking all the rules and going big, but since you are trying to convey information, you don't want to distract too much from what the reader needs to know.

When you are lining up text and pictures in your design, be intentional. Either keep things neatly lined up, or make the difference big enough so that it looks like it was done on purpose. People will notice if you are just one character space off in your alignment. It looks like a mistake. (This tip was brought to you by one of my college professors, Curt Cloninger of the University of North Carolina at Asheville.)

*Resources*
- Timothy Samara, *Making and Breaking the Grid: A Graphic Design Layout Workshop*, 2nd ed., updated and expanded
- Beth Tondreau, *Layout Essentials: 100 Design Principles for Using Grids*
- Diana K. Wakimoto, *Easy Graphic Design for Librarians: From Color to Kerning*

## OUTSOURCING CONTENT CREATION

If you have the budget to do so, it may be a good option for you to hire outside designers to create materials for your organization. These designers can do anything from writing text (copywriting) to filming and editing video, to designing print materials.

### Relationships with Designers

You can find designers online but be careful what you pay for. Cheap designers may not be creating original content for you, so someone else could already be using that logo.

It can be a time-saver to find specific designers to keep on speed dial (or e-mail) for when projects come up. If there is more than one designer you can contract with, try to find designers with distinctly different creative tastes. This year you may be looking for a hip-hop theme, but next year you may want childlike color palettes. One designer may not have quite that range, so having a wider variety of options is a good thing. Moreover, your preferred go-to designer may be busy, so having backups will help ensure that your design is created on time.

### Timing

Speaking of time, freelance designers are busy. Inquire as to how far in advance they need to consider a project. It may be several months before a design is needed. Likewise, designers with whom you form long-term relationships will cost more than someone you picked off an online "shop of designers."

*Copyright*

When commissioning designers, find out their copyright terms. Some designers may never give up the full copyright to their design and instead are granting you a license to use it within an agreed-upon manner. Others will create the design and give you full rights to it. Still others may give you full rights but ask for permission to include the piece in their portfolio. Check out the copyright guide for other issues to consider (Guide 20: "Copyright").

## GUIDE 22: Mobile-Friendly Content

If you are posting content online, you need to be aware of how that content looks for mobile device users. The increased availability of smartphones, data plans, and the ubiquity of the mobile lifestyle mean that more people are using their phones to look at your website than they were the year before. Statista.com reports that mobile phone visits made up only 0.7 percent of website traffic in 2009, while such visits were a whopping 52.2 percent in 2018.[7] These numbers will likely only increase in the years to come.

### RESPONSIVE WEB DESIGN

Responsive design is a methodology and framework for how to lay out web pages so that they look great on all devices, from a cell phone to a desktop computer. The concept was first introduced in 2010 by Ethan Marcotte.[8] Check out his book, *Responsive Web Design*, 2nd ed., for a fuller understanding of the principles and techniques involved in responsive web design. There are tools like Bootstrap (http://getbootstrap.com) which can help speed up your development process.

Designing for all screens does have a drawback in that it takes longer to code. You need to always take into account how your website will look for a mobile user. To check this on a computer, narrow your browser to its smallest width. This will give you an idea of how the website looks on a smartphone. However, the investment in responsive design pays off when you can guarantee that your site looks great no matter how your users find you.

### CONTENT

Now that your website looks great, you want to ensure that all its content is also mobile-friendly. Websites in the past loaded very quickly because they were not burdened with high-resolution photos, videos, and complicated code. For your work, you should focus on optimizing your content so that it downloads fast for mobile users. There are two main reasons why you should care. First, the user may be trying to access your website while sitting on the train with spotty cell reception. Second, their mobile plan may have a data cap on it. If your website takes too long to load, they will go elsewhere.

Images and videos should be compressed to reduce their file size as much as possible without sacrificing clarity. A smartphone's photo may be 6 MB (megabytes) in size, but you can open it in an image editor and reduce it down to 400 kilobytes. That's a 93 percent decrease in file size! Do the same for PDFs and other file types that you make available online.

## E-MAIL DESIGNS

The number of users who receive e-mails on their mobile device also increases each year. When designing your e-mails, you need to ensure that they are responsive and look great on small screens. For more tips on designing e-mails, see Guide 27: "E-Mail Newsletters."

## GUIDE 23: Diversity

Your community is made up of a diverse array of people. Your marketing materials should reflect them and their experiences. Try to include different ages, races, religions, sexualities, family groupings, differing abilities (e.g., walker, guide dog), gender, and body shapes. When looking through free stock images, it is easy to find photos of young to middle-aged, white, able-bodied people with slim figures. It is a bit more of a challenge to find free images of people who do not fit that model.

As of this writing, most stock images that draw beyond a narrow scope are found on paid sites. As a cultural organization, you may not be able to pay ten dollars or more per photo. Do the best you can with the materials you can access, and then invest in buying stock photos for promotional materials that will have a long shelf life (e.g., this year's brochure). When searching stock photo sites, you may need to search using specific keywords to find what you're looking for (e.g., a Chinese family).

Think beyond the first image that you come up with for a subject. For example, skateboarding may bring Tony Hawk to mind. Instead, think of Afghan girl skateboarders.[9]

Note: You may draw criticism for your efforts. I encourage you to push through and continue to provide a wide portrayal of how people in your community can look, engage, and interact with the world.

### Resources
- Women of Color in Tech, https://www.flickr.com/photos/wocintechchat .Creative Commons.
- Jopwell, https://jopwellcollection.jopwell.com. Attribution required.
- Tonl, https://tonl.co. Paid.
- Stocksy, https://www.stocksy.com. Paid.

## GUIDE 24: Images

Creating images from scratch is a time-consuming process. Images are created through three main processes: photographs, drawings, and graphics. You can include in your content every medium that art comes in, such as paintings or prints. For day-to-day work, however, you will probably not have the kind of time that allows you to fulfill all of your creative dreams. Instead, you need to produce work quickly and as efficiently as possible.

### PHOTOS

Photographs of your organization, users, and the impact you have on your community are great marketing materials. A well-done photo can convey more than words ever can. If your organization doesn't have a high-quality camera, a modern smartphone will do just as well.

If you don't have an artistic eye, check out photographers' portfolios on Flickr and Instagram and try to figure out what draws you to their photos. Is it the color? The subject? An eye for design is something that can be developed, though it takes time to do so. You should watch design and photography tutorials online to help you get started. Try to find out if a colleague is a talented photographer. Ask them to show you some tips.

Once you feel confident with your skills, take what you have learned about photography and train your colleagues. They may also have smartphones, so they can help you with content creation by snapping photos of interesting opportunities they come across throughout their day. Encourage them to send you the largest file size possible. Then you can use the photo in your designs. You may need to remind them of your organization's work-for-hire rules regarding the copyright of photos they share with you (Guide 20: "Copyright"). You should also check your photography policy regarding images that have users in them (Guide 31: "Photography Policies").

### STOCK IMAGES

Are you not a great photographer or designer? Are you short on time or resources to create the images you want to fulfill your dreams? Stock images are for you then! Stock images include photographs, graphs, and illustrations. You can find them for free or paid. If a stock image is listed as having a royalty, it means that you need to pay a fee each time you use the image.

Check Guide 20: "Copyright" for information on the various rights and fees associated with using other people's creative works.

*Resources*

- New York Public Library, "Public Domain Collections" (https://www.nypl .org/research/collections/digital-collections/public-domain), for photos and illustrations. Free.
- The Noun Project (https://thenounproject.com) for illustrations. Free with attribution.
- Pexels (https://www.pexels.com) for photos. Free.
- Pixabay (https://pixabay.com) for photos and illustrations. Free.
- Unsplash (https://unsplash.com) for photos. Free.

## GUIDE 25: Video

### BASICS OF VIDEO

Video will continue to grow in the years to come. You don't need an expensive setup to create videos worthy of sharing online. You can use a smartphone to capture all of your video. If you upload the video to a social media site, their app may give you some basic editing tools. Or you can upload the video to your computer, make the edits there, and then send it back to your phone via a cloud folder (e.g., Dropbox) to download. On your phone, open the desired app and make your post as usual. Some social media sites may allow you to upload the videos from a computer, but not all have a web interface.

### ADVANCED TECHNIQUES

To make your videos better, consider buying a tripod and a smartphone mount for it. This way you can eliminate shaky camera movements from your videos. Lighting is also very important. If you film a scene that is too dark, you usually cannot brighten it up without making it look poor quality. Note that some smartphones are set to make videos look best when played on them. The quality seen on a computer may be less vibrant. If you want to make more advanced edits, import your footage into video-editing software first (Guide 19: "Content").

### FILE COMPRESSION

Social media sites are going to compress your file to the smallest file size they can manage. So your video that was shot in high definition may look terrible once it is squished down to 15 MB. There are sometimes workarounds to help you manage this, but unless larger file sizes are supported, you may just have to live with your video not being as sharp as you intended. Do an online search and look for tips on how to improve the quality of your videos for a specific website.

## GUIDE 26: Print Materials

If you need to create print materials, you need to keep in mind a few important ideas in order to make your materials look their best.

### COLOR DIFFERENCES

First, print uses four ink colors to make every color. These are cyan, yellow, magenta, and black (CYMK). So when setting up your print project, try to always give it this color space. For web-only designs, use red, green, and blue (RGB), which is made up of light. Since printers don't print in light, they need the CYMK color space instead. The average viewer may not notice a difference if you accidentally design in RGB and then print it. However, when it matters, you want to use CYMK. This is an easy setting to change in your software of choice (e.g., InDesign, Photoshop).

Colors can look different, lighter, or darker depending on the monitor versus the printed page. You could buy a color calibrator to make sure your monitor is set up to the correct specs, but that is a lot of extra work and cost. If your organization has set branding colors already defined, trust those codes versus what your monitor is telling you (Guide 3: "Know Your Branding").

### IN-HOUSE VS. PROFESSIONALLY PRINTED

The different printers in your organization may print with a variety of intensities and colors. This usually happens if the ink or toner is having trouble. Try printing out the same document on every printer in your organization. Find out which machine prints the most accurate results for what you were aiming for, and then use that printer if possible. A well-run professional printer should not have these issues, of course.

Having materials professionally printed may cost more than printing them in-house, but not necessarily. If you will be doing a lot of paper cutting (e.g., for bookmarks), it may make more financial sense to have a professional printer handle that. It will save staff time, and a professional will likely do a cleaner job of cutting the paper. You should also consider going to a professional for mounting prints to foam-core backing, since this is for signs that could be up for years.

### PRINTING TO THE EDGE

When setting up your digital workspace, consider if you want your design's colors to run to the very edge of the paper or not. If so, you will want to add a bleed.[10] This means that either the paper you print on will be bigger than the final intended size so the excess can be cut off to remove the ink-free margins, or your design will be slightly smaller than the paper so the margins can be cut off.

### MARGINS

Inside the bleed line is the margin, which adds a little space between your content and where the paper will be cut (the trim line). Do not extend your content past the margin. If you do so, you risk it being cut off when the paper is trimmed to remove the excess bleed. It is generally also a good idea to not place text right up to the edge of the paper. The margin is a *suggestion* for where to stop, but a design usually looks better if text has some breathing room around the edges. I suggest a finger's width for a margin. This tip may not make sense on very small prints like a postcard.

## GUIDE 27: E-Mail Newsletters

E-mail is a powerful and effective way to get the word out about your organization's activities and services. Unlike social media, which are a firehose of information, a user's e-mail in-box is personal. Your organization can also bulk contact users via mail merge to offer a personalized experience—which cannot be done in social media.

### COST
You could try to use your organization's e-mail system, but you will likely hit limits on how many messages you can send at once. Nor can you efficiently track opens and clicks. Many e-mail newsletter providers offer a free tier for a small number of subscribers. Sending e-mail newsletters is cheap compared to social media ads. When you hit "send" on an e-mail, the vast majority will end up in your end users' inboxes. The cost per e-mail sent is very low. If you can spend money on just one thing and nothing else, choose e-mail marketing.

### CAUTION
Each e-mail client handles the rendering of e-mails a little differently. There is no industry-wide standard. So the beautiful e-mail you crafted to look great in Gmail may look terrible in Outlook. You need to make sure your supervisor and other decision-makers are aware of this fact. Your best defense is to get statistics on which e-mail services your users use. If an e-mail doesn't look perfect in a rarely used client, it is not affecting too many users. But if there is pushback, try to avoid agreeing to create an entirely separate e-mail for those edge cases. This will double your work on every single e-mail.

### MOBILE
Since the iPhone's arrival in 2007, Internet users have come to expect that they can access many kinds of online content on their smartphones. If you are able to see statistics about how users access your website, you will notice a steady uptick in mobile users over time. E-mail is the same way. So when developing your e-mails, create them to look great on mobile devices. Providers like MailChimp will show you an approximation preview of what your e-mail looks like on mobile devices.

The second factor is that users can view e-mails even when they are on slow Wi-Fi and cell data connections. But this can be slow, so try to keep your messages as light as possible. This means that you should resize your 2 MB photo to be as small a file size as possible without losing quality.

**DESIGN TIPS**

Since each e-mail client displays messages a little differently, you need to pay attention to how you lay out the e-mail and highlight the information. These tips are simple best practices:

- E-mail layouts and image widths should be no wider than 600 pixels.
- Consider using mobile-friendly e-mail templates created by your service provider. They will have tested the design in a number of e-mail clients.
- Less text is best. If you want to explain something at length, link to a website for more information.
- Use bullet points and headers.
- Have a call to action in every e-mail. You want your users to do something, whether it is registering, borrowing, sharing, or even just replying to your e-mail. Be clear about what you want them to do and then provide a means to do it (via a link or a button).
- Writing the subject lines of e-mails is an art, not a science. What works one time will not work every time. Consider using A/B testing to find the best subject line (Guide 57: "A/B Testing").

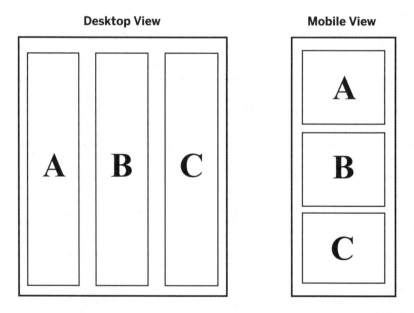

**FIGURE 5.1**
**Three-column e-mail layout as shown on desktop versus mobile view**

- The preview text is at the top left of your e-mail. It appears below or next to the subject line when viewed in the in-box. Keep the preview text short and engaging. This is not the place to put in today's date or issue number. Give a hint about the e-mail's content.
- Avoid saying "click here." This is not very accessible to visually impaired users. Their screen readers jump from link to link, so what does "click here" refer to? Instead, spell it out, such as "learn more about pandas."
- If possible, preprocess your images before uploading so they are small in file size and look sharp. You don't want blurry images.
- Images do not automatically load in all e-mail clients. You can avoid trouble by not sending e-mails that consist of just a single image with no text. If you do this, your user may receive just a blank e-mail.
- If you are writing a long e-mail newsletter to promote a single service, consider adding multiple buttons throughout the e-mail to direct the users to the action you want them to take. This way they will not need to scroll back to your link. Use this power wisely.

## MOBILE-FIRST CONTENT

The most straightforward e-mail layout is a single-column design. This reads well on smartphones. However, it is very tempting to have columns when you are designing on a computer. The trick here is to remember that columns are rendered

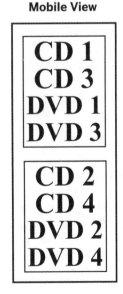

**FIGURE 5.2**
**Two-column e-mail shown in the incorrect layout**

**Desktop View**     **Mobile View**

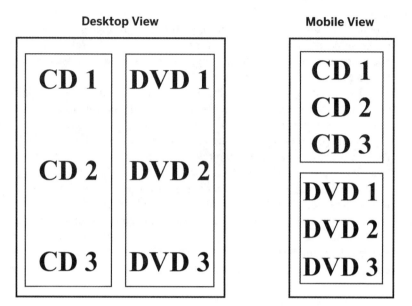

**FIGURE 5.3**
**Two-column e-mail shown in the correct layout**

left to right on small screens. Anything that is in the leftmost column (or side) of the e-mail will show up before items on the right. Thus, a three-column design of A, B, C will sit next to each other on the large screen of a desktop. But on the small screen of a smartphone, items in column B will appear below A. Then column C will appear under B. See figure 5.1 for an example.

You want to avoid adding content left to right if it will not make sense when viewed on a smartphone. For example, say you are trying to highlight your library's CD and DVD collections in a two-column e-mail. If you tried to put the CDs and DVDs into rows, your mobile user then sees an out-of-order listing of items (figure 5.2).

The correct way is to keep similar items in the same column. Then when your two-column e-mail is viewed on a smartphone, the CDs and DVDs are not inter-mingled with each other. Figure 5.3 shows how to set up the columns so they are mobile-friendly.

To avoid this issue, put items and events in columns from top to bottom, and then moving to the next column. When you look at this on your desktop, the first row will look like Monday, Wednesday, and Friday. The second row is Tuesday, Thursday, Saturday. This can be slightly confusing, but your reader will quickly sort it out, unlike a mobile user who gets all the dates out of order.

## LISTS

On the subject of whether you should have one e-mail list of recipients or several, it depends. E-mail newsletter services usually charge you based on the total number of subscribers you have in your account. If you have a separate list of recipients for each e-mail interest, you could pay for a single user multiple times. This isn't great for your budget. It is thus recommended to keep everyone in one list, and then segment it. See your service provider's website for information on how to segment a list.

The downside to having one list is that if someone gets annoyed at one e-mail segment (e.g., adults), they often just hit "unsubscribe." Then they will no longer receive e-mails from other segments that still interest them. If you had a separate list for each group, this would not happen. However, the financial cost to support multiple lists is something you need to consider.

## SEGMENTATION

When you first start sending e-mails, you may send each e-mail to every person on your list. This is okay, but it is a rookie move. You want to level up and start sending each e-mail only to people who want to see it. The content is relevant to their interest, which leads to fewer "unsubscribes." You can see segmentation in action from your local pet store when they send you coupons after you sign up for their rewards program. If you only buy cat food, they should only send you cat food coupons. Once they start sending you dog food coupons which are not relevant, you may unsubscribe, since this is not useful to you. The same concept applies to your work.

There are many methodologies for how to figure out which e-mails users want. The simplest way is to have a form on your website that offers them a few options to sign up for (e.g., children, teens, adults). Then when you send your e-mail, your e-mail service will let you choose to send e-mails about teen events to only people who signed up for teens.

Beware of offering twenty different segments on one sign-up form. The resulting long form is a real chore to read through just to subscribe to a couple of e-mails. Instead, consider adding sign-up forms to special user segments on just the website page for that interest (i.e., museum passes). The user is already interested in that topic and is more likely to be interested in e-mails about it. Check your e-mail provider's site to learn how to create a form that allows people to sign up for only a single segment at a time.

## PERSONALIZATION

The amount of personalization you can achieve in e-mails is increasing every day. The most straightforward personalization was described in the "Segmentation" section above, so users only get e-mails they are interested in. The next step is to use a user's first name somewhere within the e-mail's "to" line, subject line, or within the body of the text. This instantly feels more personal. If you are familiar with mail merge, it works similarly to that. Your e-mail list needs to have at least a first name field. When you create the e-mail, use the name merge tag that your service provider uses in your e-mail text. When the e-mail is sent out, the user doesn't see [first name] but Alejandro.

More advanced personalization may conflict with your organization's privacy and data retention policies. The way you add the personal details to your e-mails is by storing that data on your service provider's servers. This puts that data at some risk of being exposed in a data breach. Check your organization's privacy policies carefully, along with those of your e-mail provider, and research how to increase your security. If available, turn on two-factor authentication for all e-mail creators (Guide 72: "Two-Factor Authentication").

**SEND FEWER E-MAILS**
How many e-mails to send is a delicate balance. Some users can tolerate daily e-mails, but most will not. Try to be strategic with how often you send e-mails. Your organization has been invited into their in-box, so don't abuse the privilege.

If nothing else, try not to send more than one e-mail to users a day. This means that your whole organization is allotted just one e-mail to send to its user base per day. It is important to remember that users may be signed up for e-mails from different areas of your organization. If each segment or list sends an e-mail today, how many times will your users have heard from your organization within the last twenty-four hours? This increases the likelihood that they will say goodbye to all of the organization's e-mails. This one e-mail-per-day rule does not apply to one-on-one correspondence between staff and a single user.

Monitor this by having all staff notify you as to when they would like to send an e-mail to users. Schedule this on a calendar and let them know if they have the green light or not. Suggest alternative dates if you cannot let them send an e-mail out on their preferred date.

If someone sends an e-mail without notifying you, contact them and let them know not to do it again. Otherwise, you may need to restrict them to only being able to create e-mails, but not sending them. This move can be a highly political one, so use it only as a last resort.

**OBTAIN NEW E-MAILS**
You can try to recruit new e-mail subscribers by asking for their e-mail address at events, on printed materials, on a form on your website, or by offering something in exchange for their e-mail address. This last option is what you usually see on websites that offer special content only to those who share their e-mail address (e.g., free e-book). Another method is to tell users in-person that you only promote certain events or opportunities to your e-mail list subscribers. Again, check with your organization's policies to make sure that this is allowed.

Do not buy e-mail lists. There is no guarantee of their accuracy or if the accounts are real. You will likely waste money. Moreover, they may be in violation of the federal CAN-SPAM Act (Guide 28: "CAN-SPAM Act").

## OPT-IN VS. OPT-OUT

A quick way to obtain new e-mail subscribers is to ask users as they register for a card at your library. The front-line staff will need to proactively ask permission to add the user to your mailing list. This method is called "opt-in" when the users affirm that they wish to receive e-mails from you. "Opt-out" is when users are automatically signed up to receive e-mails. They will need to unsubscribe themselves. It is recommended to always explicitly ask users for their permission to sign them up to your e-mail list. Check your organization's policies regarding which method to use.

## E-MAIL AUTOMATION

Managing e-mails and personalizing them is time-consuming work. However, your e-mail platform may have tools to automate some of the work. One example is to work with your organization's IT department so that the list of new members is sent to your e-mail service provider every day to add them to your mailing list. An e-mail is then automatically sent to the new registered cardholder.

There are many options for automation and how to use it. One powerful example is to use a "drip" campaign to send a series of related e-mails over time. The drip campaign will automatically send out e-mails on your behalf. For example, you can introduce new subscribers to various features of your organization one e-mail at a time, instead of sending a smorgasbord e-mail which includes everything about your organization. With the latter's plethora of information, no single feature of your organization will stand out and shine.

Check your e-mail service provider to see which automation features they offer.

## UNSUBSCRIBES

The dreaded "unsubscribe" message you get from a user can be disheartening. You sent a carefully designed e-mail to the right user whose interest aligns with the e-mail's intent. Yet they still unsubscribed. What did you do wrong? In most cases, nothing. Take care to not take unsubscribes to heart. People unsubscribe for a variety reasons, such as they moved, they are receiving too many e-mails, they don't have time to read them, they've lost interest, or they're just annoyed.

Instead, watch for e-mails you've sent that lead to a high number of unsubscribes or bounces. A bounce is when an e-mail is sent, but for whatever reason, it does not make it to the user's inbox. You often have no control over this situation. After a number of bounces, your e-mail provider will automatically unsubscribe the user from your list. This saves you money in the long run.

If you see a big uptick in bounces, check to see if the bounced e-mails share the same e-mail provider (e.g., AOL). If so, there might be a problem with that service. Do a web search or even reach out to that company to ask what is happening. You may still not be able to do anything about it, but at least you can explain the cause. If a single e-mail has a high number of unsubscribes, check its content. Was the e-mail content offensive in some way? In that case, contact your supervisor about how to approach the situation. If the content was bad enough, your organization may need to issue an apology (Guide 68: "How to Apologize").

**WHAT TO TRACK**

The easiest metrics to track for e-mail are opens and clicks. Your newsletter service should provide you with those details. If you are not seeing any data, check that your settings allow for tracking. The users' opens are tracked by downloading a single hidden pixel graphic. When that image loads in the e-mail, it communicates back to the server that the user opened the e-mail. The number of opens can be skewed by e-mail providers which do not automatically download images, however. You may have more openers than are actually being reported.

As for what to track and when, check the weekly (Guide 51: "Weekly Tracking and Reports"), quarterly (Guide 53: "Quarterly Tracking and Reports"), and annual (Guide 54: "Annual Tracking and Reports") reports. Be mindful of your organization's privacy policies and the government's privacy laws.

## GUIDE 28: CAN-SPAM Act

There are many laws that apply to marketing. In the United States, a prominent one for you to adhere to is the CAN-SPAM Act of 2003. This law regulates how businesses can contact users via e-mail, with the aim of controlling "spam" e-mails. An overview is that you cannot e-mail people who have not given their permission for you to do so. Moreover, you cannot disguise who your organization is when you are sending the e-mail messages. If a user wants you to stop contacting them, you must stop. Otherwise, an organization that fails to meet these requirements can face expensive penalties.

Nonprofits may not need to follow the CAN-SPAM Act, but it's a good practice to obey the law regardless. Many e-mail newsletter providers will enforce the act even if you are a nonprofit.

### Resources
- Federal Trade Commission, "CAN-SPAM Act: A Compliance Guide for Business," https://www.ftc.gov/tips-advice/business-center/guidance/can-spam-act-compliance-guide-business
- Federal Trade Commission, "CAN-SPAM Rule," for the latest information, https://www.ftc.gov/enforcement/rules/rulemaking-regulatory-reform-proceedings/can-spam-rule
- Joanne Fritz, The Balance Small Business, "What Nonprofits Must Do to Comply with the CAN-SPAM ACT," https://www.thebalancesmb.com/what-nonprofits-must-do-to-comply-with-the-can-spam-act-2502412

## GUIDE 29: Web Forms

Web forms are one of the most powerful tools in your marketing kit for gathering information. They are the digital equivalent of paper forms except they are posted online. Their online nature makes it easy to share the form and gather data from people who may never step foot inside your building. They can be created for free from a number of online services. For free users, there is often a limitation on the number of form submissions or the number of forms that you can have active at one time.

Consider taking your web forms to the next level with the tips and features given below. Each idea requires careful reading, and you will need to check the capabilities of the form software that you have selected. To get help, check the forums and contact support for your software.

### BASIC FORM TIPS

- Align labels over the text fields for easier readability.
- Be wary of placeholder text. Some users may think that they cannot enter text into the field if placeholder text is there.
- Use as few fields as you can manage. Users get fatigued easily and will drop out if the form asks too much.
- If you want personal information for a survey, ask for it at the bottom of the form. Users have gone through all this work to answer your survey. They don't want their efforts to be for naught and are more likely to enter a little personal information at the end than they were at the top.
- State somewhere how you will use this data. Check to see if your organization's user privacy policy lists how long the form's data will be kept before deletion. If this is known, put it on the form page somewhere.
- Universities often have their policies regarding information-gathering go through the institutional review board. Check the policies to see if they apply to you.
- Accessibility is king. If a user cannot tab to the next field, the form software is poorly designed.

An excellent book on how to design user-friendly forms is *Web Form Design: Filling in the Blanks,* by Luke Wroblewski.

### CONDITIONAL FIELDS

You can save the user's time when filling out web forms by only showing fields that relate to that user's needs. The fields that are not needed are hidden. So if your interlibrary loan form allows the user to choose to request either a book or an article, the form will only ask for the journal's name if the user wants an article. The book-related fields are never shown. Conditional fields are an advanced use of forms. They require strict attention to detail and extensive testing to make sure everything works properly.

Among the form software that offer conditional fields are Formstack, Google Forms, JotForm, Survey Monkey, and Wufoo. Other terms that conditional fields may be called by are "conditional logic," "branching," "skip logic," or "Go to section based on answer" (Google Forms).

## FILTER FORMS TO THE RIGHT PERSON

Instead of playing e-mail operator and forwarding e-mails to the correct person in your organization, conditional fields can also ensure that book requests go to one person while article requests go to another. On the off-chance that a form goes to the wrong person, staff members can just forward the request to the right person. If staff see a lot of these errors, you should double-check your form settings.

## FORM CONTENT IN E-MAIL

When setting up e-mail notifications, you may be able to choose what information from the form submission is sent to the staff. For a book request, they may only need the user's contact details and information about the book. They may not care about the time the form was filled out. The form service provider may allow you to customize these e-mail alerts so that staff only see what they need to view.

If you are doing a combined form (interlibrary loan for both books and articles) using conditional fields, the e-mail that staff receive may appear confusing. In these cases, see if the e-mail can contain a link guiding staff to view the submission online. In either case, work with the staff to ensure that the e-mail alert they receive is clear and they know what to do with the information provided.

## SETTING UP REPLY TO SETTINGS

When your colleague gets that e-mail, the easiest way for them to connect with the user is to just hit "reply." Check your form settings to make sure that the e-mail address of the user is in the "reply to" field. Your colleague who will reply should have their e-mail address in the sender field. Again, test this a few times to make sure it works.

## CONFIRMATION MESSAGES

Consider sending a confirmation message to the user that your organization has received their submission. This notification may be sent automatically with most web form software. Within the confirmation message, you can often include the information the user submitted. This may be confusing if you use conditional fields, however. A backup solution is to instead include a thank-you message. You may also include contact information if the user has questions or hasn't heard from anyone within a specified time period.

Note: Make sure that the person whose contact information is given out knows about it. They should also have access to the submission information for that form. Teach them how to access that information and document it in a shared location that they can refer to as needed.

## ENCRYPTION

Users are becoming aware that their data can be compromised no matter how large and powerful the company is that holds that data (e.g., Yahoo!, Anthem insurance, banks). If you want to max out your security for the form, select web form software that offers encryption. This means that the data is encrypted upon submission so that the form company cannot read it.

Encryption may mean that each computer which needs to access the data must have the encryption decoder installed or stored on that machine. Otherwise, the staff user trying to look at the data will not be able to read it either. This step is one of your best options for securing your users' data. However, it is a huge hassle for staff. They will only be able to use a few computers to access the data. This limitation is frustrating when they are elsewhere and need to check the submissions. Consequently, you should approach form encryption with the expectation to get pushback from staff members.

## STYLING

If you are embedding web forms onto your organization's website, try to go the extra mile and style the form to be identical to other forms, buttons, and text on the website. You will need a knowledge of cascading style sheets (CSS) to make this happen. Don't be disappointed if you cannot make the form 100 percent seamless. Try your best to create a smoother user experience.

## TRACKING SUCCESSFUL FORM SUBMISSIONS

If you are using Google Analytics or other web analytics software, you may be interested in how many users submit a web form versus those who did not. If people stop filling out the form or never start, try to determine why not. Correcting this issue can lead to increased responses.

One way to track form completion is to send users to a new page on the website after they hit "submit." That new URL can be counted in goal-tracking within your analytics. If you don't send the user to a different page once they submit the form, the analytics software may not know the form was sent. Check your software to see how it handles goal-tracking and form submissions.

## GUIDE 30: Calendars to Develop

## YOUR GOAL

Stay on top of marketing opportunities—and help generate content when things are slow—by creating calendars.

**DIFFICULTY LEVEL** Hard.

**TIME** Hours and hours.

**COST** Free.

**WHAT YOU NEED TO START**
A place to document your findings and the ability to find the local schools' calendars.

**TOOLS**
- Internet
- Place to document responses
- E-mail

**WHAT YOU NEED TO KNOW**
This is a time-intensive activity. Some calendars are a one-time endeavor. Other calendars will need to be revisited annually, quarterly, or on an ongoing basis (i.e., snow makeup days). Additionally, your colleagues must be willing to give you a rough overview of their annual programs and themes.

**STEPS**

*Annual Programs and Themes*

1. E-mail your colleagues and ask them for a broad look at their programs and themes for the upcoming year.
   a. Ask to have each month broken out for what is going on during that time period.
   b. Ask to be alerted of any major course revisions.
   c. Is this calendar stable from year to year? If not, ask your colleagues when you should contact them for changes.
2. Copy their answers into a central location.
   a. Consider two different ways to present the information: by department and by season.
   b. Arrange the programs and themes in a list format.
   c. Look for any cross-departmental opportunities to work on a theme or project together. Inform the parties in the different departments. They may have no idea what's going on elsewhere in the building.
3. Share the big-picture calendar with interested colleagues.

*Social Media Calendar*

1. Create a social media calendar.
   a. Arrange it in a list format by month.
   b. If major holidays, religious holidays, or social media holidays (e.g., National Puppy Day) occur on the same day each year, write it as 1/1: New Year's Day.

   c. For holidays that occur on a different date each year, just list the name of the holiday.

   d. Find out appropriate greetings for the holidays. If your organization allows, post the greeting on social media.

   e. Search the Web or use the book *Chase's Calendar of Events* to find social media holidays.

2. If your organization acknowledges any religious holidays, ask colleagues that you personally know to observe religious or cultural holidays if they would look over your social media calendar.

   a. Are you missing any holidays that are significant to their religion or culture?

   b. Are there any holidays or religious observations where a greeting on social media is not appropriate?

   c. Which greeting do you use?

   d. Is there a time of day when it is better to send your greetings?

### School Calendars

1. Add the local school district and private schools' calendars to your own.

   a. Separate this from your year-to-year steady calendars outlined above.

   b. Work with staff who offer child- and family-friendly programs and themes to start promoting their resources (e.g., a craft event or museum passes) well in advance of the school closure.

   c. Pay attention to school closings that are weather-related while your library is still open. This is a great time to post and invite caregivers into the building to do something with the kids.

   d. Update this list each year. The calendars should appear online anytime from July onwards.

### Community Events

1. Create a list containing information on community events.

   a. Keep this list separate from your stable year-to-year and school calendars. Allow an exception for a major annual festival in your locality to show up on your social media calendar.

   b. If there is a hashtag that is reliably used for this event, add that to your list.

   c. Add the social media handles of the event-affiliated organizers (e.g., YWCA).

   d. Depending on your organization's policies, you may want to share posts from those events or help promote them.

**TIPS**

Create these calendars as lists. They are easier to understand than flipping through calendar pages.

Social media holidays are a great filler when you have nothing else going on.

The community events calendar is great for helping guess why door counts are low. If there's a parade going on nearby, everyone in town may be at it. Or the parade is taking up local parking spots so your users can't get into the building.

Consider adding calendars to help you track major cultural happenings like award shows and sports events. You can promote your collection of Oscar-winning films ahead of that big night.

Make sure your content-creating colleagues and department heads are aware of these calendars. They are a great central resource for understanding what is happening in the community and within your organization.

**WATCH OUT!**

When posting for holidays, you may draw complaints from those who don't think you should remark upon them. Religious and cultural holidays are big targets for these negative comments. Check out the guide in chapter 10 for strategies on how to deal with these users (Guide 67: "Handling Complaints").

## GUIDE 31: Photography Policies

You need a policy that states if you have the right to capture and use a person's likeness with or without their explicit permission. The policy protects your organization, you, and the users alike. If questions arise, you can point to the policy for guidance on how to handle the situation.

**WRITING A POLICY**

Your policy should state clearly why you are photographing or recording, what you will do with the photographs or recordings, and how people can opt-out. The policy should be posted on your organization's website. The staff should know how to respond to questions and where to direct users for further help.

**ASK A LAWYER**

This policy should be reviewed and approved by those in charge at your organization. Oftentimes, the policy needs to be approved by the board of directors. You may also need the company lawyer to verify that the policy will protect the organization from lawsuits. In these cases, your supervisor is likely the person who will handle getting the policy approved.

**KEEP IN MIND**

There's a special case to keep in mind regarding children. They may not be with their legal guardian, so the adult with them may not actually be able to give permission for that child's likeness to be used. In these cases, ask the adult if they have the full authority to make the decision. If not, ask if you may take the photo and then e-mail it to the legal guardian for permission. Be sure that you ask every caregiver if they can grant the right, since you don't want to make assumptions about who is or is not the legal caretaker.

It is recommended that you have an "I changed my mind" lenience whenever possible. If after an event, someone decides they would rather not be in a publicly shared photo, try to accommodate them in some way (by deleting it or obscuring them). However, it is not always practical to say yes to such requests. For instance, if someone is standing next to a speaker during a video, you probably cannot delete the video. You may be able to blur their face, but that is time-intensive and can be distracting, depending on the type of video.

Be kind when reviewing your photographs later on. If someone really doesn't appear in their best light (e.g., they're yawning), try to avoid using that photo in your marketing efforts.

## PERMISSION METHODS

There are six main ways to obtain users' permission to photograph or record them:

- Public place: If the likeness is captured in a public location, you may not have to ask permission.
- Post signs: State on a sign that by the user entering this location, they are granting your organization the right to use their likeness within [specific parameters].
- Crowd shots or back of heads: In circumstances where it is difficult to discern the facial features of individual people, you don't need to ask for permission.
- Only kids need explicit permission: Adults can be photographed and recorded freely, but children and teens need the permission of a guardian or caregiver.
- Verbal permission: Each person (or group) is verbally asked or advised that you are capturing photos or recordings in this location. If they don't wish to be in the photo, they should please step aside.
- Written permission: Each person who is photographed or recorded signs a form.

## HANDLING WRITTEN PERMISSION

If you need users to sign a form giving permission to use their likeness, you need to go a step further than the methods listed above. You will need to create a form which at a minimum includes key points from the photography policy, the user's name in print, their signature, the date, and a line that specifies that they are giving your organization the right to use their likeness in these specific ways. Store the permission slips in a safe location and consider making digital scans of them as a backup. Check with your organization to see if it has a records retention policy on how long the signed permission forms need to be kept.

As for the nuts and bolts of getting the written permission:

1. Print enough copies of your permission form and attach them to a clipboard. Bring along a pen.
2. Before photographing or recording, make an announcement of your intentions. State that your policy requires that anyone within the shot needs to give their written consent. Before or after the photo or recording, pass the clipboard around for people to sign the forms.
3. If this is a large group, consider bringing multiple clipboards and pens to pass around.
4. To ensure you get every person's consent form, pass the form around at the beginning so people don't walk off.

**NOTES**

1. International Organization for Standardization, "Date and Time Format—ISO 8601," https://www.iso.org/iso-8601-date-and-time-format.html.
2. Andy Klein, "Backblaze Hard Drive Stats for 2017," 2018, https://www.backblaze.com/blog/hard-drive-stats-for-2017/.
3. Eric Ravenscraft, "The Most Reliable Hard Drive Models, according to Backblaze," 2016, https://lifehacker.com/the-most-reliable-hard-drive-models-according-to-backb-1784754285.
4. U.S. Copyright Office, "More Information on Fair Use," 2018, https://www.copyright.gov/fair-use/more-info.html.
5. National Eye Institute, "Facts about Color Blindness," 2015, https://nei.nih.gov/health/color_blindness/facts_about.
6. Carl Straumsheim, "Berkeley Will Delete Online Content," 2017, https://www.insidehighered.com/news/2017/03/06/u-california-berkeley-delete-publicly-available-educational-content.
7. Statista, "Percentage of All Global Web Pages Served to Mobile Phones from 2009 to 2018," 2018, https://www.statista.com/statistics/241462/global-mobile-phone-website-traffic-share.
8. Ethan Marcotte, "Responsive Web Design," 2010, http://alistapart.com/article/responsive-web-design.
9. Kat Lister, "Skateboarding Makes Afghan Girls Feel Free," 2015, https://www.vice.com/en_us/article/wd7n5z/skateboarding-makes-afghan-girls-feel-free-881.
10. InDesignSkills, "InDesign Basics: What Is a Bleed and When Do I Use It?" 2015, www.indesignskills.com/skills/indesign-bleed.

*chapter* 6

# Staff Training and Interactions

YOU HAVE ALL YOUR MARKETING SYSTEMS IN PLACE, BUT HOW DO YOU GET the staff to follow them? When new people are hired, how do you get them trained so everyone works consistently? How do you prove your expertise and worth to your colleagues? This chapter answers all these questions and provides the nitty-gritty of how to get the information you need for success.

Before you start, check out Guide 1: "Getting Staff Buy-In." Hopefully, after all those meetings and talks, you have gained your colleagues' trust.

## GUIDE 32: Build a Network of Support

**YOUR GOAL**

If this marketing work is all new to you or you have just arrived at your organization, you may feel a little out of place. Your supervisor can help you feel more grounded, but you will need to make friends and find support. Fortunately, you have already met the key people you need to get your job done.

**DIFFICULTY LEVEL** Intermediate.

**TIME** Ongoing.

**COST** Time.

**WHAT YOU NEED TO START**

You will need time to form these connections in your organization. Before calling on your new creative partners—that is, your colleagues—the first time, make sure you understand your job (Guide 2: "Outline Your Job Scope") and what marketing options you can offer the staff (Guide 4: "Make an Inventory of Marketing Offerings").

**TOOLS**

- Note-taking tools

**WHAT YOU NEED TO KNOW**

Since you met with your colleagues while getting staff buy-in, you already have an idea of who can help you out (Guide 1: "Getting Staff Buy-In"). These may be the department heads, but more likely, it is whoever has been doing marketing there already. Look for the creative types who write website events, make bookmarks, and create social media posts. They have a wealth of knowledge that you should learn from. They can also support your initiatives.

**STEPS**

*Working with Individuals*

You should schedule informal meetings with your creative partners to ask about their projects. Look for small ways you can help them out. If possible, meet up with them on a semi-regular basis just to stay aware of what is happening throughout the organization. Like any friendship quest, try to pick up little tidbits about them and be friendly. You want them to trust you as an understanding person to work with who appreciates their brilliance.

If you have the time and budget to do so, consider taking each key department partner out for coffee. Ask them more in-depth about how they work. You may uncover someone who has a background in marketing or a related field. If so, lucky you! This person is now your best friend.

You should empower as many colleagues as possible to create their own marketing materials and designs. If they are competent, they can take a great burden off you. The best people to encourage in this way are those who are willing to listen to your advice. In an ideal situation, you will only need to spot-check and give them feedback on how to improve.

Let go of having full control. Going along with the idea above, you need to recognize that others will not do things exactly the same way you would do them. If you have established good branding guidelines, that will define the creative canvas within which they can work. For example, if your organization has a strict no 1990s clip art policy, that helps nip out the worst designs from the outset.

*Working with Groups*

You should try to attend meetings in other departments every now and then. Get yourself put on their agenda. Take up to twenty minutes to tell them:

- Here's what is coming up across the organization that affects publicity.
- Reminders of anything they should do between now and the next meeting you attend.
- Ask what they have that needs any publicity.
- Do they have any questions for you?

Likewise, if there are big, organization-wide status update meetings, try to attend one of them. Take this as an opportunity to refresh everyone on the big marketing pushes coming up. Share a couple of big highlights and insights found from your work. Ask if there's anything you need to know.

After all group meetings, go over your notes, digest them, and take steps towards enacting them. Then schedule those tasks out on your calendar. If you can do this immediately after the meeting, that is even better.

## TIPS

Attending to all these relationships can take up a lot of your time. But these partnerships are valuable. They will be your first line of support and backup if needed.

Keep your meetings with individuals limited to 30 to 60 minutes at a time. If you are part of a larger organization-wide meeting, your speaking portion may be less than 5 minutes. Keep to the highlights and need-to-know information.

When attending group meetings, you may not get any tips to help you pad out your content creation calendar (e.g., what service/resource should I promote next month?). If that happens, take it to mean that whatever you do will be fine by them. They had their chance to steer the marketing ship at the meeting. If the staff later have comments about what they'd prefer you to promote, consider switching paths, if this would cost you little time or effort to do so. You don't want to hurt their feelings, but you also need to keep up with the strategies you have already settled on.

## WATCH OUT!

There are more idea generators in your organization than just the officially recognized ones. If you don't talk with other people in each department, you may miss great insights and concepts. You should form good relationships with as many colleagues as possible by demonstrating a willingness to listen and discuss their ideas. Your organization's next golden idea could just be waiting for someone (like you) to listen to it.

## GUIDE 33: Educational Resources

### KEEP YOURSELF UP TO DATE

Whether you have a marketing background or not, you will want to know the latest trends, techniques, and laws in the marketing field. Online marketing changes from week to week and software updates occur often, so you need to keep up with what is happening.

But don't get too overwhelmed by trying to learn everything at once. Start by signing up for one e-mail newsletter (MarketingProfs is my daily go-to) and go from there.

## BOOKS

A Book Apart (https://abookapart.com/products) publishes books that are primarily geared to web designers and coders. They also have books for creative types about project management, business management, and understanding users. Their authors are among the most respected in their fields.

Barbara Diggs-Brown, *The PR Styleguide: Formats for Public Relations Practice,* 3rd ed. This book is expensive, so look for an e-book version. It will help you develop public relations documents.

Sara Eatherton-Goff, *The Content Strategy Planner: An Uncomplicated Guide to Simple Content Marketing.* Aimed at bloggers, this book helps you develop your long-term promotions.

Steve Krug, *Don't Make Me Think, Revisited,* 3rd ed. This book is the gold standard in learning how users approach the Web. Krug emphasizes simplicity and helping people make snap judgments from your design and text.

Rosenfeld Media (https://rosenfeldmedia.com/books) publishes a variety of books to improve your design thinking, understand users, learn new technology, and manage products.

Sara Wachter-Boettcher, *Content Everywhere: Strategy and Structure for Future-Ready Content.* The author's engaging voice explains the importance of well-structured writing platform systems in helping content producers to write better.

Susan M. Weinschenek, *100 Things Every Designer Needs to Know about People.*
————, *100 More Things Every Designer Needs to Know about People.* These two books by Weinschenek are fun and accessible ways to learn a lot about how people think and how you can influence them.

## E-MAIL NEWSLETTERS AND WEBSITES

With most e-mail newsletters on marketing, you should just glance at the topics and read only what you are interested in. Most of these newsletters can be looked through in five minutes.

Before & After Magazine (www.bamagazine.com) is a monthly e-mail that features new design techniques and case studies on how to improve designs.

GoodUI (https://goodui.org/fastforward) is a weekly e-mail which offers tips on better A/B testing with lessons learned from real-world tests (Guide 57: "A/B Testing").

Hubspot (https://blog.hubspot.com) offers paid tools to help monitor users, generate leads, and more. They send a lot of e-mails, but they are full of tips and offer free content-management tools on their website.

Litmus (https://litmus.com/blog) is a premium e-mail service, but they offer great reports and tips via their blog. Sign up for the newsletter to get their best tips. Check out their "Resources" page for further help.

MailChimp (https://mailchimp.com/resources). This leading e-mail newsletter service is affordable. They also offer a variety of newsletters to help you grow as a marketer and a designer, and they provide fun peeks behind the scenes at their workplace.

MarketingProfs (https://www.marketingprofs.com/newsletters/marketing) is a daily newsletter offering their top marketing links of the day. The links are to a mix of articles, infographics, paid classes, and podcasts. There is usually one true gem every day.

TechSoup (https://www.techsoup.org/support/articles-and-how-tos). Learn about new technologies and techniques aimed at nonprofits.

## ONLINE CLASSES

Bonnie Biafore, "Project Management Foundations: Small Projects." Online class, Lynda.com, 2013. https://www.lynda.com/Project-Management -tutorials/Project-Management-Foundations-Small-Projects/612167–2 .html. This is recommended by Cecily Walker (Guide 8: "Time Management").

Primer (https://www.yourprimer.com) is an app to help you grow your marketing and business skills with bite-sized lessons.

Skillshare (https://www.skillshare.com) is an affordable, video tutorial website aimed at short, single-topic lessons that are taught by both professional teachers and hobbyists.

## PODCASTS

Neil Patel and Eric Siu, "Marketing School with Neil Patel and Eric Siu," podcast audio (https://marketingschool.io). Each episode is five minutes or less and is released daily. The primary focus is on digital marketing and tools.

John J. Wall and Christopher S. Penn, "Marketing over Coffee," podcast audio (https://www.marketingovercoffee.com/first-time-visitors), offers a weekly twenty-minute discussion on traditional and new marketing techniques.

## RELATED FIELDS

Don't limit yourself to resources tied to just marketing, communications, and public relations. Expand your knowledge to include user experience, service design thinking, graphic and web design, and psychology.

## GUIDE 34: Keep Staff Involved

Part of the art of marketing is making sure the right people know the right thing at the right time—and this includes your colleagues. They're busy people, so you'll need to do some legwork to keep them informed and involved.

### SHARE INFORMATION

The first thing is to create opportunities for staff to learn new marketing trends, what other departments are doing, and how they can be more collaborative in your organization's outreach efforts. You want to encourage them to share information not only with you, but also with each other.

### PHOTO SHARING

Encourage the staff to take photos and save them in a shared location. You can reuse these photos for annual reports, social media posts, and e-mail marketing. If your organization doesn't have a photo policy (Guide 31: "Photography Policies"), make sure to push for one, and make sure that all staff are aware of the rules.

You may also need to arrange training for the staff to learn how to take usable photos that have great lighting, a clear focus, and interesting subject matter. If your organization has a semiformal staff education process, go through that venue so you can get multiple people trained at once.

### GO CROSS-DEPARTMENTAL

When reviewing publicity requests and the upcoming months' programs and events, are there complementary programs or services that are being offered in different departments at the same time? An example of how to do this is for summer reading. In public libraries, this may be an entire library-wide effort as you develop programs for children, teens, and adults. Yet, because it's such a busy time, no one may consider what other departments are doing at the same time. You can help out by doing the following:

- A couple of months before the start of the development process for next summer's programs, contact each department. Ask them about their plans. What is the theme?
- As an outsider to their efforts, look for opportunities where the departments can pull together on similar programming themes.
- Give the departments a common deadline which will give you plenty of time to publicize their events.
- If your library contracts an outside designer, make yourself the point of contact for that person (Guide 21: "Design"). You only want the designer hearing from one person so that it all stays streamlined.
  - Note: Try to keep your e-mails threaded for each individual project with the designer. That is, don't create a brand-new e-mail when you want to ask how things are going with a single project. This will save

you a headache later when you're trying to find all the messages to that designer.

- Create publicity plans for each department—which you'll use for your own planning purposes (Guide 15: "Publicity Plans"). When scheduling your publicity time line for a cross-departmental theme like summer reading, make sure to give each department's big programs time to be the solo star for a few days. This helps avoid feelings that you are promoting one department's program at the expense of others.

## ATTEND MEETINGS

You're a busy person. As such, you may not get much face time with those colleagues who aren't sending you publicity requests. One way to connect with entire departments is to attend their meetings every now and then. You'll get an opportunity to learn about their problems that might never come up in conversation otherwise, and you'll learn about projects they forgot to mention to you (how can you tie those into what someone else is doing?). You can share what organization-wide departments are doing from the 30,000-feet view and share any new marketing trends and news with them. For example, let them know about a new newspaper in town.

These in-person meetings are valuable, since a lot of information-sharing comes up just while talking face-to-face. In order to send someone an e-mail, you have to recall something—often on your own—and then sit down and compose the message and explain what you're trying to get across. But by seeing people face-to-face, you can work together to brainstorm without those boundaries.

As for which meeting to attend, see if you can go to a quarterly one where they'll be discussing the next several months. You may be put first on the agenda, which can cut off opportunities for you to get those good off-the-cuff ideas as the department discusses their upcoming work—especially if you are pushed out of the room once you say your piece. Even so, see if you can get a rundown of the agenda ahead of time so you can ask specifically about items that may be of interest to you.

## E-MAIL NEWSLETTER FOR ONLINE MENTIONS AND NEWSPAPERS

A big hit at my library has been my weekly write-up of what's happening on the Web and in print surrounding the organization. I pull together social media interactions, blog mentions, and where and when we appeared in the local newspaper. The newspaper step is easier if you have only a weekly paper, not a daily one. Check out Guide 58: "Marketing Report for Staff" for a full description of this e-mail newsletter.

## MANAGING SCHEDULES

You may find yourself spending a lot of time managing your colleagues' schedules. While technically I report to a supervisor and have no one who reports immediately to me, in reality, at least two staff members from each department require me to manage their time. These are the people whose time I have to watch:

- Anyone who contacted me with a publicity request
- Department heads whom I ask about what is going on in the near future
- Fund-raising and the administration on money-raising efforts
- Those in charge of annual programs or services. Contact their responsible person well ahead of time to ask if the program or service is happening this year, and what publicity they will need.

By managing my colleagues' schedules, I keep people on task to get their work done so I can get my end of the project done. This often means:

- Creating a publicity plan for their project with due dates, and assigning each item to a specific person
- Delivering the marketing plan to the person and making sure they understand what it means
- Contacting colleagues to ensure they send their items in on time
  - This is usually done by e-mailing them a reminder a few days in advance of the deadline.
  - Make clear to them what happens if they don't get their items in when needed.
- If they don't have the items in on time, you then have to ask them for it directly.
- If they drop the ball entirely and bring everything to a halt, you have to deal with the fallout from that. You can only do so much on your end, and you may need to go to their supervisor for backup.
  - Staff are ultimately responsible for their projects. If they don't do their work, you can't do it for them. This may wreck your schedule, but you can't make items appear that don't exist.
  - Don't beat yourself up over someone else's failure to deliver.

To help keep your sanity, always set deadlines for staff several days to a week in advance of when you absolutely need something. Your colleagues are just as busy as you are, and you never know what has happened on their end. They'll be grateful that they get just one more day to catch up.

## GUIDE 35: Staff Training Now and in the Future

To maximize your marketing impact, you need to establish procedures to get staff trained now and in the future.

### ESTABLISH POINT PEOPLE

You will likely be in contact with numerous colleagues throughout your organization. In order to help meet some of the demands and expectations placed upon you, you should find a point person within each department. This is ideally a colleague who has a vested or personal interest in the organization's marketing, branding, or how you are all perceived. These colleagues truly care about how the community sees and interacts with the library. If they already have marketing chops, all the better. If not, work with them to ensure that they know the branding guidelines, basic design concepts, and information about the community that their department targets (Guide 3: "Know Your Branding").

The point person's job is to take pressure off you and help hold their immediate colleagues accountable. Whenever any new publicity items are created for public viewing (photos, flyers, e-mails, social media, etc.), the point person should be the one to give it a quick review. For non-point people who are excellent and confident in their medium (e.g., writing), the point person may not need to carefully scrutinize each thing they produce. But the point person is the one to look for typos and give quick feedback. A point person would help with the staff management aspect to ensure that their colleagues are delivering items to you on a timely basis (Guide 32: "Build a Network of Support"). Look for a point person in the assistant head of the department.

If you don't have these point people, you may find yourself in a situation where you are personally responsible for reviewing each and every item that is created. You don't have that kind of time. Instead, help out your (formal or informal) point person by providing them with templates and examples of what good publicity items look like. Encourage the point person to contact you when they need another pair of eyes to review something. Send your point people thank-you cards or give them a bar of their favorite chocolate every now and then. They are doing you an enormous favor and should feel appreciated.

### TRAINING CURRENT STAFF

Depending on how your organization is structured, you may have regular opportunities to set up training sessions for the staff. You can show staff how to use your publicity submission system (Guide 5: "How to Gather Marketing Requests"), show them what the branding guidelines are (Guide 3: "Know Your Branding"), and share new marketing techniques. Ideally, these groups would be small, with no more than five people. This gives them time to play off each other and remind themselves of issues they're unclear on solving, and this size is manageable enough for you to create a personal connection with each attendee.

What you teach staff depends on what you are responsible for (Guide 2: "Outline Your Job Scope") and what publicity items you offer (Guide 4: "Make an Inventory of Marketing Offerings"). The training that I have offered in my own library includes how to:

- Add book lists and events to the website.
- Organize and name files.
- Write for the Web.
- Take, edit, and share photos.
- Understand the organization's audiences (Chapter 7: "Who Are Your Users?").

Afterwards, send the attendees an e-mail outlining what you went over and linking to where they can find more information. You may need to go to people's computers and bookmark the publicity submission form for them (Guide 7: "Ingest Form Setup"). Show them where the form is located and how to use it.

## TRAINING NEW STAFF

If department heads have an on-boarding checklist for new hires, ask to be included. Don't go into details on what you will be training the staff. Each hiree will have their own responsibilities which does not translate to a single training checklist. This is what you want to happen:

- To be listed on the training checklist
- The department head to provide the introduction for you and the new hiree (an e-mail serves this well), just so you both know that you need to set up a meeting
- Understand what the new hiree will be responsible for, so you can decide what to teach them

On your end, you should create a checklist of what to tell each person who will be working with you. For those with whom you will have general contact:

- Give an elevator speech of what you do.
- Briefly describe the community they will work with.
- Outline some ways you can help them get the word out to the public about their department's offerings.
- Encourage them to ask you questions, ask for help, and send you new marketing ideas.

For those you will work more closely with, share the above and:

- Branding and writing guidelines
- Specific details on marketing areas they will work within or be responsible for (e.g., a social media account)
- Where to submit marketing requests
- Where to find logos and templates

- How to name files and where to save them
- The workflow for getting publicity for their needs
- Which items need to go formally through the submission process, and where just a quick e-mail will suffice
- Explain how you will work with them
- When they need to tell you about their marketing needs

Ideally, all of the above has been documented in some shared location which the new staffer can easily access. I recommend printing out the branding and writing guidelines. Then hand-write with big text how far in advance they need to submit requests. They're going to be overwhelmed with all the new information that is coming their way. If nothing else, the advance notice deadline is the most important information you can communicate.

For both groups (current and new staff), follow up on the training session by sending them an e-mail outlining what you went over. Invite them to ask for clarification or for help. Then you may need to go to people's computers and bookmark the publicity request form for them (Guide 7: "Ingest Form Setup"). Show them where it is located and how to use it.

## GUIDE 36: Managing Assistants

### HOW TO MANAGE ASSISTANTS
If you are fortunate, you will not be the sole person responsible for managing marketing for your entire organization. Assistants will ease your burden and allow your department to do more. Your impact within the organization will also increase, since assistants can free you up to attend more face-to-face meetings. And by seeing your colleagues in person, you build stronger relationships.

If you don't have any assistants, you may still be able to find help among your colleagues (Guide 32: "Build a Network of Support"). Or you can use some free or cheap resources to expand your output (Guide 24: "Images").

*Hiring*
Congratulations on being lucky! It's now time to hire assistants. Since this is not a how-to book for managers, I will just give you some brief ideas to help you find the right people. For these examples, I am assuming that you're setting up your department from scratch. The suggestions here are applicable for other situations as well.

First, check your budget and determine how long you can hire someone for. While a year-round employee is a dream come true, you may only have enough funding to hire help during the busiest time of the year. Be up-front about the time span in your job ad. If allowed, save the time of job seekers by including the salary.

Second, where do you need help? Be honest when evaluating your own skill set and the needs of your organization (Guide 2: "Outline Your Job Scope"). You want to find people who complement your weak areas. You may be an excellent project manager, but need help in writing the perfect copy, in knowing when to jump on social media trends and when to abstain, or in designing brochures. If you are a one-person operation, you may be trying to do all of the above and more on your own. If so, you're not alone. Many marketing people at cultural organizations are doing it all by themselves.

Once you know which task needs to be filled, run the numbers to see if you have enough work for a person to focus on just that task. If not, what else would you have them do? Include that in your job ad so you can get the great copywriter who is also a graphic designer.

Third, post your job ad in a variety of locations. Depending on your budget and whether the position is year-round, you may want to try a more national search. The big association job lists (e.g., the American Library Association's JobList at https://joblist.ala.org) may charge a fee. Think outside the box of where the people you're interested in may be looking at job ads. Designers may be at AIGA Design Jobs (https://designjobs.aiga.org), while computer programmers may be at Stack Overflow (https://stackoverflow.com/jobs). You should also try posting to specific job sites and electronic discussion lists, such as the Asian Pacific American Librarians Association, in order to get greater diversity in candidate applications.

When hiring, talk with your organization's Human Resources officer. This person will give you the guidelines you need to adhere to, ethical concerns, and how to stay within legal requirements. If you are hiring a designer, webmaster, or programmer, look at their portfolio of work.

### Assistants I Wish I Had

My peers at other organizations in the locality often include these jobs among their teams: social media, graphic designer, and e-mail/web designer. By contrast, I work as a one-person operation. But I can think of many assistant positions which would make our marketing even better. In the meantime, it's just me filling all of the roles listed below and more:

- Computer programmer/coder
- Copywriter
- E-mail designer
- Graphic designer/illustrator
- Liaison to other departments
- Print designer
- Public relations expert
- Social media maven
- Someone to answer e-mails
- Audience researcher
- Webmaster
- Video editor

### When You Don't Have an Assistant

If you cannot hire an assistant, you can still leverage other resources to lighten your load.

- Build partnerships with other creative people in other departments so they can help work on their own marketing needs.
- Hire temporary designers for a project.
- Use public domain or affordable visuals. For example, to create the Darien Library's Bookfix logo (shown in figure 6.1), we licensed an image from NounProject.com and then altered it.
- Create templates and use them for similar projects.

**FIGURE 6.1**
**Darien Library's Bookfix logo**

## MEETINGS

If you have an assistant, set up a regular meeting schedule with them. Weekly or biweekly is the most effective schedule. Structure the meetings to include these items:

- Updates on what they're working on
- Anything they need help with
- Your list of things for them to do
- Any bigger organization news they should know
- Ask if there's anything else they would like to discuss

## QUICK FEEDBACK

You should also make yourself available for quick review and feedback sessions. Your designers and writers may get stuck in how to convey something. Or they are simply out of ideas. Establish a communication channel (in-person drop-ins, e-mails, chat, etc.) and let your assistant know that they can get a quick response from you that way between scheduled meetings. Most of the time, these reviews will only take a couple minutes. Then your assistant can get back to work.

## REMOVE OBSTACLES

As a manager, part of your job is to remove obstacles that are stopping your assistant's work. Your assistant needs information from others in your organization in order to do their work.

Keep in mind that a lack of communication may exist because the person in another department who is responsible for giving information doesn't know that they are the point person (Guide 35: "Staff Training Now and in the Future").

Their supervisor may have forgotten to tell them this basic fact. Likewise, your colleagues may be away unexpectedly. Keep your tone cheerful but firm and remind them that marketing can't share their great work with the public if you don't know what that work is—and well ahed of time.

## TIME AND PROJECT MANAGEMENT

Most of your time and project management of your assistant's work will happen in your scheduled meetings with them. However, you can also keep on top of things by adding your assistant's tasks into your own project management system (Chapter 4: "Set Up Project Management"). Depending on the software you are using, you may be able to directly input tasks and assign them to that assistant. Bonus: You can also assign due dates in most software.

If using software, you can also establish a culture of assistants writing notes about their task's progress. This can seem a little like micromanaging, but it helps you to stay on top of issues as they come up. Your assistant goes to their task and then leaves a comment about their trouble spot. Then they tag you to send you a notification. You can quickly respond. Then at the end of the week, you can relax knowing that everything is progressing nicely.

Likewise, if you notice that someone has not touched a task in a while, you can send them a quick reminder in that task that the first draft is due soon. Depending on your managing style and the assistant's receptiveness, this may be just the quick reminder that they need. Your assistant may have gotten sidetracked by another department's unscheduled request for help.

Overall, in your management style, try to find the right match between your needs and those of your organization. Some managers and employees are better hands-off, while others need a little more guidance. Each approach is valid. Be flexible and adjust your managing style to the needs of the people you trusted enough to hire.

*chapter* 7

# Who Are
# Your Users?

THERE ARE A VARIETY OF WAYS TO LEARN ABOUT YOUR USERS. YOU CAN ASK them directly, infer information based upon their behaviors, or use third-party data resources (e.g., the U.S. census).

## GUIDE 37: Target Audiences

Your **primary audience** is the one that you are trying to reach with any marketing effort. Thanks to your research, you know what they are interested in, what they need, how they like to be communicated with, and what problems they would like to solve.

Your **secondary audience** are users who happen to also see your marketing efforts and are often in the category of "they would be nice to recruit." For example, a program on constructing family trees would have a primary audience of genealogists. Local historians are not the same as genealogists, but they too might be interested in new research methods. Therefore, they would be considered a secondary audience.

## GUIDE 38: Respecting Privacy

### A WORD ON USER PRIVACY
If you are trying to learn about your users without directly asking them for their explicit permission, you can run into privacy concerns. Some information professionals

advocate for knowing nothing about who uses their services and resources. As marketers in a cultural organization, you may lean in the opposite direction, but stop just short of creating a customer relationship database to help track your organization's interactions with individual users. Or maybe you want all the data you can get.

The key here is to investigate your organization's privacy policies and have frank conversations with your supervisor and others on your group's stance. You don't want to run afoul of stated or implied rules regarding user privacy. If you are part of a professional organization, you may also have ethical concerns as part of your membership's beliefs. Likewise, various laws may apply to user privacy.

This guide provides sources that you can consult for information regarding your users. Your organization's policies should be followed. If you have any qualms, check out just the simple surveys (Guide 41: "Simple Surveys") and program attendance (Guide 42: "Program Attendance vs. Door Counts") guides, which discuss the more privacy-neutral avenues for learning more about your users.

### Resources

- Data Privacy Project, https://dataprivacyproject.org
- American Library Association, "Library Privacy Checklists," www.ala.org/lita/advocacy
- American Library Association, "Library Privacy Guidelines for E-Book Lending and Digital Content Vendors," www.ala.org/advocacy/privacy/guidelines/ebook-digital-content
- Theresa Chmara, *Privacy and Confidentiality Issues: A Guide for Libraries and Their Lawyers*
- Jason Griffey, Sarah Houghton-Jan, and Eli Neiburger, *Library Technology Reports: Privacy and Freedom of Information in 21st-Century Libraries*
- Nicole Hennig, *Library Technology Reports: Privacy and Security Online: Best Practices for Cybersecurity*
- American Library Association, "Privacy Tool Kit," www.ala.org/advocacy/privacy/toolkit

## CODE OF ETHICS

The professional organizations of librarianship and archives treat user privacy in their codes of ethics. These codes are also backed up by federal, state, and local laws. What information can be stored, shared, and accessed depends on these factors, as well as the organization's own privacy policies.

As a marketing professional, it is tempting to collect and use all the user information that you can obtain. But one of the principles behind our professions is to respect the right of our users to enjoy and use our collections without worrying about whether anyone knows what they are researching or enjoying (within legal bounds). However, we are also under immense pressure to compete with commercial ventures. Those operations can provide more personalized experiences than we can, thanks to our fields' emphasis on privacy.

You should consult the privacy policies of your organization and ask about its legal obligations in order to understand what you can (and cannot) do. Find out what targeted marketing methods you can use and still stay within the organization's policies and the law. As a shorthand, if you are interested in expanding your marketing options to users, use an opt-in method to get their consent (Guide 39: "Confirmation Methods"). The following text shows how three professional organizations handle user privacy.

### Three Associations' Codes of Ethics

The American Library Association's "Code of Ethics" states: "We protect each library user's right to privacy and confidentiality with respect to information sought or received and resources consulted, borrowed, acquired or transmitted."[1]

The Society of American Archivists' "Core Values Statement and Code of Ethics" has a lengthy statement. It ends with, "Archivists respect all users' rights to privacy by maintaining the confidentiality of their research and protecting any personal information collected about the users in accordance with their institutions' policies."[2]

The American Alliance of Museums' "Code of Ethics for Museums" does not explicitly discuss user privacy as a tenet. It does say:[3]

> But legal standards are a minimum. Museums and those responsible for them must do more than avoid legal liability, they must take affirmative steps to maintain their integrity so as to warrant public confidence. They must act not only legally but also ethically.

## GENERAL DATA PROTECTION REGULATION (GDPR)

As of this writing, the GDPR had just gone into effect on May 25, 2018. The ways it will change the Internet and companies are still unknown. The GDPR is a European Union (EU) law that regulates data privacy and protection for people within the European Economic Area.[4] Just because your organization may be outside of the region does not mean that you're exempt from the consequences of breaking the EU's law. EU citizens who live abroad are still protected under this law. You should seek legal advice to understand how the regulation affects your organization.

How the GDPR will affect marketing is also unknown. The days when any data gathered can be used forever are now gone under this regulation. This book is not a guide on how to do marketing under these rules. The following information was learned from Hubspot. The major GDPR considerations are:

- Your organization must protect data to the highest level.
- Be transparent and specific about how you are using the data you're gathering and how long you will keep it.
- Users can more easily access their "right to be forgotten."
- User data needs to be downloadable in a common format.

### Resources

- Hubspot, "GDPR Compliance," https://www.hubspot.com/data-privacy/gdpr
- Hubspot, "What Is the GDPR? And What Does It Mean for the Marketing Industry?" https://blog.hubspot.com/marketing/what-is-the-gdpr

## GUIDE 39: Confirmation Methods

When dealing with user engagement and privacy, you have two main ways to obtain users' permission. These confirmation methods grant you the right to share a user's name, photo, likeness, comments, and so on within your marketing materials. In addition, these methods determine how you may contact users—if they allow you to do so. You will need to deal with this in developing your user privacy, e-mail, social media, and photography policies, among others (Guide 31: "Photography Policies").

### OPT-IN
In the sentiments of this author, and on the basis of many conversations with other library professionals, opt-in is the preferred method to obtain confirmation. You want your users to actively confirm that you can use their likeness or information. See Guide 40: "How to Collect User Information" on ways to get users' permission.

### OPT-OUT
This method involves posting notices in the building, on the website, or other online accounts. Often the notice states something along the lines of: "By visiting these premises, using these resources, or registering, you are giving us permission to . . ." The notice may be prominently displayed, or it may be deemphasized. Users who wish to be excluded need to take action to have themselves removed from any use of their likeness or information.

## GUIDE 40: How to Collect User Information

As a marketer, you cannot succeed without learning about your targeted audiences. There are a number of privacy factors to consider, as well as legal rulings and ethics. You can gather data on users directly by asking them, or indirectly by using other resources (Guide 38: "Respecting Privacy"). Many of these tools are discussed in detail in guides 41 through 47 in this chapter (see below.)

### QUESTIONS TO ASK YOURSELF
Before collecting user data, you should answer the following questions:
- Why are you collecting this information?
- How will you use the data?
- Who will have access to the data?
- How will you securely store this data?
- How long will you keep this data?
- Is this question needed to obtain the data?
    - This is especially true for demographic data or personally identifiable items like name or birthdate.

**COLLECTING DATA DIRECTLY FROM THE USER**
- Ask them in person (Guide 41: "Simple Surveys")
- When they register or become a member
- Evaluation sheet or feedback form
- Sign-up for a program
- Reply to an e-mail or social media post
- Diary studies, which usually involves users documenting their own processes and approaches when attempting to solve a problem or use a service, that is then shared back with the researcher.

**COLLECTING INDIRECTLY WITH ANONYMIZED DATA**
- Social media stats (Guide 46: "Social Media Insights")
- Website analytics (Guide 47: "Other Ways to Learn about Users")
- URL shorteners (Guide 56: "Shortened URLs")
- Census (Guide 44: "Census")
- Reference questions
- Collection or resource use statistics

**COLLECTING DATA INDIRECTLY FROM THE USER**
- E-mail interactions if a tracking pixel is being used (Guide 27: "E-Mail Newsletters")
- Observational studies
- Mapping (Guide 45: "Mapping")
- Program attendance or door counts (Guide 42: "Program Attendance vs. Door Counts")

**COLLECTING DATA INDIRECTLY FROM COLLEAGUES**
- Staff interviews (Guide 1: "Getting Staff Buy-In")
- Staff-sourced user groups (Guide 43: "Staff-Sourced User Groups")

**USER EXPERIENCE RESOURCES**
The field of user experience (UX) also offers dozens of research techniques. UX is a broad term that encapsulates an organization's efforts to understand users' needs, how users think about things, and how the group can provide a better, more appealing, or efficient way of addressing the needs of the user.

- Elizabeth Goodman, Mike Kuniavsky, and Andrea Moed, *Observing the User Experience,* 2nd ed.
- Steve Portigal, *Interviewing Users: How to Uncover Compelling Insights*
- "Practical UX Methods for User Experience Professionals," http://practical uxmethods.com
- Christina Rohrer, "When to Use Which User-Experience Research Methods," 2014, https://www.nngroup.com/articles/which-ux-research-methods

# GUIDE 41: Simple Surveys

**YOUR GOAL**
If you want to know what your users want and are interested in, you don't have to guess. You can just ask them. Each survey method described here is simple to implement and gives immediate results.

**DIFFICULTY LEVEL** Easy.

**TIME** 15 to 60 minutes.

**COST** Free, or the cost of making some copies of the survey.

**WHAT YOU NEED TO START**
Decide what you are trying to find out.

**TOOLS**
- Two pencils or pens
- Paper
- Clipboard

**WHAT YOU NEED TO KNOW**
This project can be intimidating if you are shy. The first method is considered a guerrilla tactic, since you are catching people on the go instead of formally inviting them to a place and time to participate. This survey method is best for quick, on-the-spot information-gathering. You could also develop a simple survey and share it via e-mail or social media. Both methods are described below.

**STEPS**
Both simple surveys that are described below share a common beginning, so start at the first section below, and then go to the "Guerrilla" or "Online" instructions below to complete your project.

*Develop Your Survey*
1. What do you want to know? Be specific. Your topic should also be useful knowledge for your organization.
2. Design a short survey of no more than five questions. Try to make most of the questions open-ended and phrased in such a way as to invite more than "yes or no" responses.
3. Share your survey with a few colleagues to see if it's clear and if it's likely to get the kind of information you seek.
4. Depending on whether your survey will be done in person or online, read one of the next two sections (below).

### Guerrilla Survey

1. Type your survey up and print it out. Leave blank space between the questions so you can write.

2. Place it on your clipboard and bring two pencils or pens in case one breaks.

3. Practice an elevator speech to include your name, why you are seeking the user's input, and if you are offering a token of thanks, say that. Keep this speech short. Don't ask the user's name unless you are asking the user to commit to a more intense survey later on.

4. Ask at least five people their thoughts. Be friendly and courteous. Thank people whether they agree to take the survey or not. Make sure to do the writing yourself so you can read it later.

5. Afterwards, thank the user and give them your token of thanks. Then go seek your next participant. Make sure to look for a variety of people to survey.

6. Tuck your completed survey under the pile on your clipboard.

### Online Survey

1. Open the form software of your choice and design your form (Guide 29: "Web Forms").

2. Use paragraph boxes to allow for long answers.

3. Decide on a time frame for how long you are gathering responses. If there is a specific deadline, include that in the instructions.

4. Choose a method to distribute your survey: e-mail, website, paper signs, or handouts that link to the form.

5. Distribute the link to the online form.

### Afterwards

1. When you're done, review the responses and look for immediate patterns or gems. You don't need to do a deep dive if you are looking for one particular item. Keep the surveys (or scan them) to refer to later, since they are a valuable resource to you.

2. Share what you learn with others.

### TIPS

To get more people willing to talk, offer a small token to thank them. If your organization has a café, a cup of coffee is popular—especially early in the morning, on cold days, and with tired students.

Consider adding a "staff area" to the survey form so you can note the location, date, and time the survey was completed. If the location where your survey was taken may be of interest, include that. Users in that area are likely using resources in a specific way (e.g., caregivers taking their charges to storytime), which can help you understand the context of why the user was in the building.

Seek out people on different dates and times, since the users who are present change throughout the week. For example, teens may not be in at 10 a.m. during the school year. The needs of the people you see now may differ drastically from those on another day or time.

Ask people to elaborate on what they mean if you don't understand what they've said.

Bonus: If you have a population that speaks a different language and a staff member who speaks it, recruit that person to approach those users.

Another survey method is to ask someone to try and accomplish a quick task in front of you (e.g., how to search the catalog). If doing this, recruit a colleague to take the notes while you focus on the user.

## WATCH OUT!

When put on the spot, users may not remember to say anything that they wish your organization did better or differently. Moreover, since you work at the library, the users may be reluctant to say anything negative about it.

Sometimes you will not gain any useful insights from users. That's okay. On the other hand, you may get a quote which can be used anonymously on your marketing materials. Or even a nice comment to improve a colleague's day.

The response rates for online surveys are often low. It could take days or weeks for answers to trickle in.

## GUIDE 42: Program Attendance vs. Door Counts

### YOUR GOAL
People are coming into your building, but are they showing up at your programs?

### DIFFICULTY LEVEL Intermediate.

### TIME Three hours.

### COST Free.

### WHAT YOU NEED TO START
This guide assumes that you have some historical data regarding how many people enter your building and how many attend each program you offer.

### TOOLS
- Spreadsheet
- Access to program attendance numbers and door counts

**WHAT YOU NEED TO KNOW**

This data can be a little slippery to work with, since there are many factors that can influence a user's decision to come to a program. Was it a holiday weekend? Was there a big sports game or awards show on TV during the program? Was the weather too perfect or too dangerous? This information is a guideline to help you see overall patterns for your organization.

Figure 7.1 (page 108) is a simplified six-month version of the table you will be developing.

**STEPS**

This spreadsheet looks very impressive to your colleagues. If you share it with administration and department heads, they may see new ways to look at door counts and program attendance once it is separate from the rest of the stats collected.

*Set Up Your Spreadsheet*

1. Locate the historic statistics on program attendance and door counts to see if this information exists. If yes, continue.

   a. Create a new spreadsheet.

   b. Name your columns like so, starting in the second column:

      (a) First month in your calendar year (tip: use abbreviations to save space)

      (b) Second month in column C, third month in column D, and so on.

      (c) Total per Year

      (d) Average per Month

      (e) Notes

2. Starting with your second row, name the following rows:

   a. First year to input (however your organization defines a year. This may be 2020 or 2019–2020. This can be the most recent or the oldest. I recommended the newest.)

   b. Whatever broad categories for program attendance that your organization uses (e.g., adults, teens, children). One per row.

   c. # of Programs

   d. Door Count

3. At this point, copy your rows from the Year row to the Door Count row to create a quick template.

4. Paste this in the row right below your first Door Count. Change the year to the next (or previous) year.

5. You can paste your template down the page for as many years as desired.

   a. If your organization had a fairly recent big change (like moving to a new building), consider that as your stopping point. Consider adding the year prior to the move too, as a comparison to the change between old and new.

| | July | Aug | Sept | Oct | Nov | Dec | Total per Year | Avg per Month | Notes | Notes |
|---|---|---|---|---|---|---|---|---|---|---|
| **2018-19** | 40,174 | 45,212 | 41,530 | 43,155 | 40,177 | 36,598 | 246,846 | 41,141 | Attendance total row | |
| Adults | 2,411 | 3,008 | 2,761 | 3,582 | 3,639 | 2,908 | 18,309 | 3,052 | | |
| Teens | 97 | 108 | 187 | 212 | 65 | 74 | 743 | 124 | | |
| Children | 2,764 | 2,984 | 3,618 | 2,413 | 3,555 | 2,681 | 18,015 | 3,003 | | |
| # of Programs | 91 | 110 | 168 | 147 | 151 | 87 | 754 | 126 | | |
| Door Count | 34,811 | 39,002 | 34,796 | 36,801 | 32,767 | 30,848 | 209,025 | 34,838 | | |
| **2017-18** | 4,610 | 6,021 | 6,503 | 6,264 | 7,076 | 4,587 | 35,061 | 5,844 | Attendance total row | |
| Adults | 2,317 | 2,902 | 2,861 | 3,782 | 3,481 | 2,108 | 17,451 | 2,909 | | |
| Teens | 113 | 88 | 151 | 196 | 77 | 65 | 690 | 114 | | |
| Children | 2,180 | 3,031 | 3,491 | 2,286 | 3,518 | 2,414 | 16,920 | 2,820 | | |
| # of Programs | 87 | 103 | 141 | 157 | 145 | 97 | 730 | 122 | | |
| Door Count | 34,622 | 38,753 | 34,381 | 35,624 | 29,874 | 26,749 | 200,003 | 33,334 | | |

FIGURE 7.1
Example of a six-month program attendance and door count spreadsheet

b. Otherwise, stop at around ten years of previous program attendance and door counts.

6. Apply background colors to each year's worth of data to make it easier to read.

    a. Use the lighter colors instead of the dark ones. The text should be legible.

    b. Make the year row a slightly darker color than the monthly raw data numbers.

    c. Avoid applying red to one year's data and green to the one immediately next, due to red-green color blindness. Do the same with blue and yellow (Guide 21: "Design").

    d. You can make the Total per Year and Average per Month cells all the darker color of the year row.

### Enter and Add Up Your Data

1. Input the raw data numbers from your program attendance and head counts into each cell. Be careful to check your data as you input it.

2. For the Year row, you want to add up only the total attendees for that month's column for that year. Use formulas to make this easier.

3. How to add numbers in Microsoft Excel and Google Sheets:

    a. Type *=SUM(*

    b. Click on the first cell in that's month's column. Hold down the Shift (PC) or CTRL (Mac) key, then click on the last program category's cell. This will select all cells in-between. The formula will be two cells with a colon in-between. For example: *=SUM(A2:A13)*

    c. Type *)* to finish.

    d. Tap *Tab* to go to the next cell. You should have a sum total number now of all the attendees for programs that month. Double-check that with a calculator to make sure.

    e. If it works, hover over the cell with the formula in it until a square appears in the lower-right corner of the cell. Left click and hold, then move your mouse to the right. Let go when you come to the last month in your year.

    f. Tap *Tab* to finish.

### Finish the Table

1. Annotate your data by adding comments to individual cells or writing in your Notes column. If you have the information, note when there was a department head change, a long leave of absence (e.g., maternity leave), or why that's an abnormal month (e.g., during midterms month you may have more teens than usual). You want to note down major players whose absence or start date made a big impact on the organization.

2. At the bottom of the data, add up the Total per Year and Average per Month columns. Label your rows:

   a. Total Attendance
   b. Total (how data is broken down into categories; e.g., children, teens, adults. Use as many rows as needed.)
   c. Total Door Count

3. Add up your two columns for each row.

   a. Type  = SUM(
   b. Hold down the shift key and click only on the needed cells. In the cell you are adding your total into, there will be commas between each cell. For example:  = SUM(A14, A20, A26)
   c. Type ) and then hit *Tab* to finish.
   d. Do a spot check to make sure that one sum is correct.

### Create a Summary Table

1. Set up a mini-table to quickly show changes from year to year.

2. In the first row, enter the table's title.

3. Label the columns:

   a. Years you covered in the main table (written as 2022 or 2021–2022).
   b. Attendance
   c. Door Count
   d. Notes

4. The final row is your totals. Double-check that they match the numbers in your raw data.

5. You can use a cell reference to call those numbers up for future ease. Then any changes you make in the raw data will automatically update in your summary chart. Do an online search for "cell reference" to get the latest formula for your software.

### Data Analysis

How the data can be crunched and made sense of will depend on how your organization will use it. The data can be useful when discussing additional funding needs (e.g., the door count has gone up X percent in the last two years). For this guide, you want to see if there are any correlations between the door count and program attendance. If the numbers are low, you could then look for new ways to market to targeted groups.

If there are any serious outliers, highlight those cells in a bold way (e.g., red, yellow, and green). Add a comment or enter in the Note field as to why you selected that data to be looked at more closely.

**TIPS**

You can combine this information with e-mail click-throughs to see a funnel of users' commitment and level of interest (Guide 27: "E-Mail Newsletters"). To do so, track how many people clicked from your e-mail to your website's event page. Then compare that to how many people actually attended the program. Doing this on a consistent basis over time may reveal patterns and issues. For instance, if 150 users indicated an interest in astronomy by clicking on it in an e-mail, but only 10 people showed up in person, what was the cause of the disconnect?

You will not get that answer handed outright to you, but it highlights an area to investigate. Work on this in conjunction with the programming staff. Once you know your average ratio between click-throughs and program attendance, you can start predicting how many chairs you will actually need, or if another person will be needed to help manage the crowd. These ratios, when split across different categories of programs, can help you look for opportunities to grow, or to remove resource-draining events that are not of interest to your community.

If you don't have historical knowledge as to when people in your organization left or were absent, consult with colleagues to see what they remember. If your organization has an internal newsletter, the information might be in there or in a shared personnel calendar. This data hunt can become overwhelming. If you can't find out staff changes, that's fine. Try to be mindful of them in the future. Knowing when there was a staff change or leave of absence can reveal why program numbers drastically change. For example, if the teen librarian is on maternity leave for several months, the number of teen programs may drop considerably during that time. Or if someone with fresh energy is hired, they may revamp program offerings, which could lead to increased program attendance and door count numbers.

Add a note in your spreadsheet for where you found your raw data.

**WATCH OUT!**

Go back and spot-check your counts to make sure that everything comes out right.

Remember to update this spreadsheet on a regular basis. Remind your supervisor and other colleagues of its existence.

## GUIDE 43: Staff-Sourced User Groups

**YOUR GOAL**

If you don't have time to do hours, weeks, or months of in-person user interviews, is there another way to learn about your community? You can learn much about how your organization is used by the community from the staff who work directly with them every day. They can share their knowledge by grouping users into categories with common characteristics.

**DIFFICULTY LEVEL** Hard.

**TIME** 8 to 10 weeks.

**COST** Free.

**WHAT YOU NEED TO START**
You'll need the goodwill and cooperation of your colleagues to take on this time-intensive project. They will be contributing substantial time on your behalf as they try to categorize the people they work with every day into representative groups.

**TOOLS**
- Spreadsheet
- Printer
- Index cards
- Markers
- Sticky notes
- Pen/pencil

**WHAT YOU NEED TO KNOW**
The best source of information about your community is those staffers who talk to a diverse and representative range of people. This group of people is made up of those who use your organization's offerings. But by talking with the staff alone, you will encounter biases and perceptions that may not hold up to scrutiny. You should go into this project with the knowledge that you are getting a reading of the community by how the staff perceive them. You can supplement this discovery phase by conducting simple surveys with actual users (Guide 41: "Simple Surveys").

Finally, many staff members may not see the bigger picture of the community as they work in their focused area. Your work here will allow them to see how they function as part of a whole. They may even discover that people who they thought were only in their area may also be engaged in other ways.

**STEPS**
After reading through this guide, talk to your supervisor to make sure you have the institutional support to take on this endeavor. At the end of it, you will be able to share the staff-sourced user groups with the whole organization. The staff-sourced user groups can help with the development of new programs, marketing, and outreach to underserved populations, and help staff better understand the importance of their own role.

After completing this project at my library, departments were able to better target their programs toward the groups they were trying to reach. Staff could also evaluate their offerings to see which groups they were not engaging with at that time and take steps toward rectifying that oversight. As well, it was clearer to staff that users have multifaceted needs and seek services or resources elsewhere in the building—not just within their own department.

For example, a caregiver may also visit the computer lab in order to print because the children's area does not offer computers for adults. Once in the computer lab, the caregiver may encounter users who are not as understanding toward a crying child. Once a discovery like this is made, the children's area can then consider adding computers for adults in order to better serve caregivers without sending them elsewhere in the building. Prior to the staff-sourced user groups exercise, the children's area may have been unaware of this need. Only through an overarching look at how user groups move throughout the building and the offerings they partake of, can opportunities for improved services like this be realized.

### Gathering Data

1. Start a new task in your project management setup to track this project with deadlines and who has responded (Chapter 4: "Set Up Project Management").

2. Create a master spreadsheet which you will send to each department or area of your organization. Make a copy for each department.

3. The columns of the spreadsheet should be:

   a. User Group: Staff may give straightforward names for their groups of users (e.g., Genealogists) or whimsical names (e.g., Passionate Museum Lovers)—which is part of the fun.

   b. Age Range: You may discover surprising demographics, such as teens showing up in unexpected places.

   c. Gender Ratio: This helps you find opportunities to market to new segments of your users.

   d. Occupation: This is a demographics question that helps you guess at what kinds of programs or services may be of interest to those users (e.g., homemaker, retired, remote worker, business person, student, or child).

   e. Resident: Depending on your organization, it may be important to know if you can offer services (e.g., e-books) to some segments but not to others. This is the hardest question.

   f. How Do They Reach Us? Are people engaging with your organization in person, via e-mail, phone, social media, or some other way?

   g. What Are They Here For? Think of things that you offer that are not a simple resource (e.g., meeting like-minded individuals in your library).

   h. What Resources Do They Use? These may be databases, books, Wi-Fi, staff assistance, and so on.

   i. What Are They Looking For That We Don't Offer? How are you disappointing this group? Often this is something that cannot be changed, like more parking.

4. What to tell department heads about the project:
   a. Don't stress out over these user groups too much. This is not scientific.
   b. Explain that you are looking for a best guess for each column.
   c. Think of the users they interact with as groups with shared characteristics and goals.
   d. Be specific with details, but don't create too many user groups. Ten is about right for each department.
   e. A person may go into more than one category (e.g., they come to crafting events and use computers).
   f. Ask your colleagues how long they believe it will take for their department to brainstorm this document. Expect it to take 4 to 6 weeks due to holidays and vacations.
5. With regard to item f, make a note on your project management setup for each department as to when to expect their response. Schedule a reminder for yourself to check in a week before the department's due date.

### Compile the Data

1. Once the spreadsheets are all returned, now comes the hard part: looking for similar patterns and compressing these fifty (or more) user groups into a manageable number.
   - I took 106 user groups and stripped them down to seven core user types to match the seven design elements in our logo.
2. Create a new spreadsheet and add a worksheet for each question. This spreadsheet is where you will gather all your raw data that was submitted.
3. The columns in each worksheet are Data Asked (e.g., Age Range), Count (how many groups are in this data range), Audience Affected (the name of the user group), and Notes.
4. Then do the time-consuming work of adding every user group's information into each worksheet.
   a. For example, with *Gender Ratio*'s first column, write in a different row the ratios given by the staff. Several user groups will likely have the same guessed ratio. In other worksheets, put in this first column the attributes that more than one group shares (e.g., for Services We Don't Offer, you may have unique items like Tutors and Playground).
   b. In the Audience Affected column for each row, write down the name of each user group as given by your colleagues. All of these user groups will be in one cell together.
   c. Add an acronym for the department that supplied the information in order to help you remember who submitted it. For example, Front Desk would show up as (FD) written after the name of the user group, such as Direction Asker (FD).

  d. Once you have added all the user groups for a row, count the quantity and add it to the Count column.
- This is helpful for showing that three of five service desks report directional question-askers.
- Add any notes, such as if a department forgot information about a user group in that category.

5. Once all your data is gathered together, look through each spreadsheet for common qualities and outliers. These common qualities will be the basis for your final user groups.

### Make Your Groups

This step is helpful for those who are visual or who like to physically move index cards around.

1. Cut the index cards in half in order to set a limit on the amount of data you will write on each card.
2. At the top of the card, write the name of the user group.
3. On the bottom left, write Location and then the Department where this user group can be found.
4. On the bottom right, you may use highlighters to draw a rough bar chart comparing the gender ratio.
5. Decide which key things you need to highlight about each group. Sometimes you may not need to write anything if you are very familiar with a particular group. Other times you may need to jot down facts like what they want or how they reach you. Don't try to put in all the information. This is just a snapshot. You can refer to your spreadsheets for detailed data.
6. Set out all your index cards around you. Begin to look for patterns.
  a. How you choose to categorize users into similar groups depends on what you're really looking for from this exercise. For me, it was: what do people want from my library? Your own curiosity may be focused on how you are not meeting people's needs.
  b. A user group may be represented in more than one department (e.g., *Users of the Collection* are in the Children's Library, Teen Area, and Adults).
  c. Stack these cards on top of each other.
  d. Add a sticky note on top with a brief name/description of what those user groups have in common (e.g., Parents).
  e. Some user groups may go into more than one category. You will need to make a decision about these.
  f. The beginning of this task is easy, but at the end you will likely have a couple dozen user groups who have unique needs or use resources drastically different than the groupings you have already identified.

7. How to handle those outliers:

a. Are they truly unique? Someone who is here just to use a specific resource can be grouped with others who are also focused on using specific resources and not doing anything else. Don't focus on the resource they are using, but on the fact that they are here to focus on a resource and not attend programs for example.

b. Do you believe the user group description is an accurate depiction of their needs? If you suspect the data may be incorrect, feel confident enough to toss it out. Or seek out someone who matches those characteristics and ask them a simple survey to tease out any information that may help you find out what they really want from your organization.

c. If a user group keeps nagging at you because it cannot be accounted for elsewhere, you may want to tentatively keep it as its own unique category.

8. When you are done sorting your cards, check again to see if you can further compress any categories together. You want to try and keep the categories to a minimum. Ideally, you would be able to easily recite the categories from memory later on.

9. At this point, you may know more about the overall community of your organization than anyone else. Congratulations! You are seeing the big picture here and are ready to start teaching others.

### Share Your Discoveries

If you are going to give a presentation, consider combining this exercise with some of the other guides in this "Who Are Your Users?" chapter.

1. How you choose to present the data will depend on your ultimate goal, and what you are trying to communicate, as well as your design skill set.

2. One method for sharing your groups is:

a. Gather visuals to help represent your users. Use diverse imagery.

b. On the first slide, write the group name in a large font size. Then add a list titled "Groups Identified by Staff." This helps people understand the underlying structure of who and what went into creating each group. Your colleagues will also appreciate seeing that you are representing their work—by name!—on the slide.

c. On the second slide, keep the name of the group in a large font size. Then add sections for Characteristics, Contact (how the group contacts the library e.g. e-mail only), and Locations (where the group can be found in the building or online). Optional: Include age range or gender information if pertinent.

d. Under each section, use as few words as possible to get your point across. Don't try to add every single desire under "Characteristics." Refer back to your raw data to find the most popular interests.

e. In your speaker notes, write up any bonus information that you would like to convey about each group; for example, any outliers that have an additional need.

3. When giving your presentation, stress:

   a. This is not scientific research, but a collection of organization-wide observations of your community.
   b. Thank everyone for their involvement in the project. It was a time-consuming process for all of them.
   c. People's needs change over time and they may move between groups.
   d. A person may be in more than one group at a time.
   e. Discuss the limitations of your work and how it may be further tested and developed.
   f. Make suggestions for how these user groups can be implemented within the staff's work.

4. Ways the information may be used:

   a. It can act as a benchmark to see how user needs are being met.
   b. You or other staff can check the raw data to look for ideas on how to improve services and collections.
   c. Look for opportunities to have cross-departmental projects to serve user groups they have in common.
   d. You can improve the way different users get in contact with the organization. If one group prefers e-mail contact, look for ways to deliver information better in their preferred format.

**TIPS**

This project can stretch out over several months, depending on the time of year when you are attempting to do it. Departments may wish to wait until certain staff members are available to participate. Try to keep the project moving forward, but don't stress too much if it's taking longer than planned.

Keep your real due date for the returned spreadsheets a week or two after you expect them to be back.

Staff may prefer to fill out the information as a text document. Be flexible about this and just copy the data back into your spreadsheet later on.

Sometimes you may need to change the name of a user group to make it clearer (e.g., take a fanciful name and simplify it to one that is understandable at a glance).

**WATCH OUT!**

This project is overwhelming. Schedule out plenty of time and breaks for yourself.

Your colleagues may have a tendency to focus only on users that they see and forget those who only visit online.

The staff are likely not as knowledgeable about people who don't visit or use your organization's resources.

Be careful about organizing groups under demographics. Seniors and teens may both want to find other people to hang out with. This desire is not unique to either group.

Since you are not relying primarily on first-person contact for this project, be careful about drawing assumptions that are too broad. Likewise, if you interview a few representatives of a particular group, remember that they cannot speak in absolute terms about everyone or even about most people who fall into that category.

In spite of everyone's hard work on this project, it may go no further, or the data may have no further applications. If nothing else, you now have a large-scale project to add to your resume.

## GUIDE 44: Census

Censuses are a wonderful source of data about your community and its neighborhoods. The best-known census, the U.S. Census, is taken every ten years, but the Census Bureau also conducts dozens of additional surveys in-between for businesses and individuals.[5] States may also do their own surveys. If you are outside the United States, check your country and regional governments to see what information is available to you.

### DATA DISCOVERY USING CENSUS DATA
There are hundreds of things you can learn from a census:

- Income and neighborhood data
- Changes in populations over time
- Ages and families
- Education level
- Languages spoken
- Types of industries located nearby

### WHERE TO FIND CENSUS DATA
American FactFinder (https://factfinder.census.gov) is the U.S. Census Bureau's website which provides information in a user-friendly way.

Data USA (https://datausa.io) provides census information in an easy-to-understand and attractive format. Their ready-made charts can be included in an in-house presentation to share information. Town data is compared to state-level data in order to show how your community compares to the state at large. If your town is small, Data USA may use data from a neighboring city as their dataset in some examples.

*Resources*
- MIT Libraries, "Census and Demographic Data: International Data," https://libguides.mit.edu/census/international
- U.S. Census Bureau, "Economic Census: Uses of Data," https://www.census.gov/programs-surveys/economic-census/guidance/data-uses.html
- U.S. Census Bureau, "Data Tools and Apps," https://www.census.gov/data/data-tools.html
- U.S. Census Bureau, "Public Libraries Survey," https://www.census.gov/econ/overview/go1800.html
- U.S. Census Bureau, "Academic Library Surveys," https://www.census.gov/econ/overview/go1700.html
- U.S. Census Bureau, "State Library Agencies Surveys," https://www.census.gov/econ/overview/go1900.html

## GUIDE 45: Mapping

Visuals are a powerful tool for understanding lots of data and for making arguments. If your organization collects any location data on users, you can take that raw data and turn it into a map. Check your institution's privacy policies, since even having raw street addresses may be considered a privacy violation.

### DATA DISCOVERY USING MAPS

Since visualizations are so powerful, they can help you discover information that may not be clear from just viewing a spreadsheet. If you combine address information with census data, you can draw even more powerful inferences.

- How many unique addresses are in your database? Use this to find the average number of users per household.
- Are there streets or neighborhoods where few users are located? If so, consider sending mail to that area touting what your organization can do for them.
- Where are members of a specific category of users located (e.g., book groups, retirees)? How can you do outreach to them in their local area?
- If you use late fines data, are there neighborhoods where it is common to have high fines? What may be the cause of that? For example, no return box nearby, a lower-income community which may have trouble making it in during open hours, or large highways which hamper walking access to a branch or a return box.
- If you include expiration date within your information, you can try to figure out why former users are no longer visiting your organization. Did a competing organization (commercial or nonprofit) open up a location nearby that is more convenient for them to visit?
- You can target mailings about children's programming and services to households that are located near schools or day care centers.

## CLEAN UP THE DATA

Whichever format your user data comes in, you may need to clean it up to make it usable. You can do this in spreadsheet software. Making your data usable will likely be the longest and most frustrating part of your mapping work. Your cleanup work may include:

- Removing personal identifiable information (e.g., names or e-mail addresses)
- Standardizing spellings and converting acronyms to spell out the term (e.g., St. to Street)
- Removing excess spaces before words in your cells
- Combining columns together

If you want to make your data filterable, you will also need a column for that information; for example, whether the user is a donor or not. Clean up your data from a copy of it and keep the original in a safe place in case you need to start over.

## GEOCODE THE DATA

Your user database likely does not provide latitude and longitude coordinates, which are used by mapping software to unambiguously identify locations. You cannot plug in a street address. Therefore, your spreadsheet will then need to be geocoded. This step can be done by a variety of online providers for free or at a paid rate.

- U.S. Census Bureau Geocoder, https://www.census.gov/geo/maps-data/ data/geocoder.html. This is free and can geocode up to 10,000 addresses per day.
- Texas A&M Geoservices, http://geoservices.tamu.edu/Services/Geocode. This is paid and provides a variety of tools.

Check the geocoder's documentation to ensure that your data is in a format that it can understand.

## MAPPING DATA

Now that your spreadsheet has been whipped into shape, you are ready to put it on a map.

Google Fusion Tables was a great free tool which could do the geocoding and mapping for you, but it will be discontinued in late 2019.[6] As of this writing, Tableau is another popular mapping option. It offers paid and public (free) versions. You can visualize your data in multiple ways, with maps being just one design output. The disadvantage of Tableau Public (https://public.tableau.com/en-us/s/) is that your map is posted online and cannot be completely hidden from the open web. However, you can turn off the others' ability to download your data.[7] The advantage of Tableau is that your maps and charts will look fantastic.

## WHAT TO DO NEXT

All those hours of work to clean up your data and then present it on a map will pay off now. You can either embed the map into a website, take a screen capture to put in a presentation, or give web access to your map to others. The fundraising arm of your organization can also use your maps to help them refine their efforts. Check out how you can do mailings to target those individual households that would be most receptive to hearing from your organization (Guide 47: "Other Ways to Learn about Users").

Are you interested in learning other data visualization tools? Check out the open-access textbook "Data Visualization for All" (https://www.datavizforall.org).

## GUIDE 46: Social Media Insights

### YOUR GOAL

Who are you talking to on social media? Find out so you can share with them the content they want from you.

### DIFFICULTY LEVEL Intermediate.

### TIME Ongoing.

### COST Free.

### WHAT YOU NEED TO START

Access to the organization's social media accounts at the administrative level.

### TOOLS

- Social media accounts
- A place to take note of insights (Guide 13: "Personal Knowledge Base")

### WHAT YOU NEED TO KNOW

This guide cannot give you detailed information on social media platforms, due to how much websites will change between when the guide is written and the time you read it. This section is an overall look at what kinds of information you can glean from the data. Access to some platforms' analytics data may cease before you read this guide.

### STEPS

1. Log into the administrative account of your organization's social media profile.
2. Many of the most popular sites share some analytics about how well your posts are doing (e.g., Facebook, Instagram, Twitter, YouTube).
   - You may need a business account to see detailed audience information.

3. The information provided differs with the platform. YouTube focuses more on gender and age demographic information, while Twitter shares your followers' interests (e.g., tech news), consumer buying styles, occupation, and net worth.

  • Most of this information is based upon guesses based on a user's online habits.

4. What do you do with this information? You will be doing some broad generalizing based upon your audience's demographics and interests.

   a. You can promote a women's business group on a platform where your audience is predominantly female.
   b. You can post more GIFs and comics, and capitalize on social media trends for younger audiences.
   c. You can adjust your organization's voice to be more casual or formal.
   d. If you want a service or resource to be used more by a certain demographic, write your copy to appeal more to their needs and post it to the social media platform they may be most active on.
   e. Some platforms will share when your followers are more likely to be online, so you can post when peak users are on the website.
   f. You can discover if your followers speak another language.
   g. You can find out how far your posts are reaching in the world. During vacation times, you may notice more hits from abroad if your community tends to travel overseas.
   h. If many followers are retired, are parents, or work from home, you can consider when they would be more available to attend programs.
   i. You can change how you communicate with the audience based on their post interactions (e.g., text, photos, and videos).

5. You can take the information and use it to communicate with your colleagues about how to best reach their targeted audience.

## TIPS

Good content marketing involves taking the same piece of information and presenting it to different audiences in a format they find appealing. For instance, a book review may work as a video on one social media platform, but an image of a quote with a photo of the book on it may work better somewhere else. You still have one source of information, but how you share it changes based upon the audience.

You can also ask your followers point-blank what they want from your social media account or why they followed you.

## WATCH OUT!

It cannot be stressed enough that this demographics information, and your conclusions about which marketing ideas appeal to them, are based on generalizations.

Women aged 25–40 are more likely to have a child in the house compared to a 60-year-old woman, for example. So you should advertise snow day programs to those who are more likely to find the information useful and on a social media platform where they are more likely to see it; that is, women who can take their kids to the library because school has been cancelled for the day.

Generalizations can also be harmful if not handled with care. Men are also parents, so they may want to know about the snow day programs too. You don't want to neglect to share information that could be of interest outside the stereotypical expectations of what people want to know about.

## GUIDE 47: Other Ways to Learn about Users

### GOOGLE

There are more Google tools you can use to learn about users than can be covered in this guide. Google offers a variety of free online classes to help you get the most out of its tools. Its learning tools are not restricted to just web-based offerings, but also include the Google Primer app. If you have a few minutes, you can learn a new mini-lesson in business and marketing each day.

### GOOGLE MY BUSINESS

Some information about your organization will be auto-generated without your initiative, but you can keep up on trends by setting up a Google My Business account (Guide 66: "Google My Business"). A profile for your organization has likely already been created. If you take charge of it, you can scoop up all that data and keep the information accurate with a Google My Business account. However, even if you don't create an account, you can learn a lot just by googling your organization's name. This information will give you a quick view of how users are interacting with your organization and how you appear to them.

With the Google My Business account, you can get specific numbers as well as information about search results, how often driving directions were requested, who called you from one of Google's interfaces (search or Maps), and how many website visits there were. Take the numbers provided and compare them to your own internally captured numbers. How close are they? Are there any major discrepancies between them?

### GOOGLE ANALYTICS

If your website uses Google Analytics (or any other kind), you can gather additional data on your website's visitors. How the General Data Protection Regulation will affect this kind of data will continue to change in the future (Guide 38: "Respecting Privacy"). At present, you can learn keywords that were searched which led to your website, how users moved from page to page, where a user was before they came to your site, how often this type of user returns to your website, as well as lots of information about the technology they are using, and a general idea of where they are located in the world. This is just the bare minimum of what you can learn from website analytics data. If you combine it with A/B testing, heat maps, and other web analytics tools, you can discover what kind of content works best for your audiences (Guide 57: "A/B Testing").

## MYBESTSEGMENTS

If you love infographics, Nielsen provides consumer-level data and analytics with its free tool MyBestSegments.[8] This tool pulls partially from census data to help build demographic and lifestyle data about communities. If you go to the site's "ZIP Code Look-up" and enter your target area, you can learn about the general preferences, lifestyles, economics, and media consumption habits of a particular zip code. The colorful charts can be screen-captured and added to a presentation.

You can use information from MyBestSegments to help you plan how to market to a small geographic area (i.e., a zip code). Online advertising tools like Facebook can target by area code, so make sure your ads are going to the right people. For example, if you want to look for potential donors, check for the zip code that has more disposable income. Cross-check that information with the "ConneXions" tab to see how those groups get their information. If they are not heavy online users, consider ads by doing a physical mailing, advertising in a newspaper, printed signs in the community, or radio ads.

## ATOZDATABASES

If your organization offers access to AtoZdatabases, you can obtain a list of people who just moved to your town. This offers a gold mine of opportunities for marketers, but it can also raise privacy concerns. However, this information is publicly accessible. AtoZdatabases includes information about new movers and homeowners. The information is pulled together from several other databases. You can export the results for your own convenience.

### How to Use the Information

If your organization has the time and funds, you could schedule a regular period to pull these new residents' names and addresses from sources like AtoZdatabases, and then send them a postcard inviting them to come in to the building. If you send a postcard, make sure it includes a few highlights that would be really meaningful to them. If there are not too many new residents, try handwriting at least their name on the card for a personal touch.

## OTHER WAYS TO FIND NEW RESIDENTS

Does your town hall or neighborhoods offer welcome wagons? If so, try to slip something in their welcome basket about your organization. A similar venue is local realtors. If you go this route, try to establish up-front how often you should drop off new flyers, packets, and so on to their office. These groups are offering a great opportunity for you. Make it easy for them and keep them stocked up with publicity materials.

Look for events offered around town that are aimed at new residents. Your organization may be able to set up a booth and go meet people in-person.

Kindergarten registration is also a good time to look for potential new users. Contact the local schools to see if your organization can set up a table there. If you do this, make sure to bring along little pieces of swag for the new students. Even something as simple as a colorful pencil would be appreciated.

### Mailings

If your organization has a print budget, you can send targeted mailings to different neighborhoods to promote your services. Check with your local postal services to find out how you can restrict mailing to a certain locale. The U.S. Postal Service offers some mapping tools through its Every Door Direct Mail service (https://eddm.usps.com). You can find out how much it would cost to send mail to a particular area, use census data to target specific households (e.g., ones more likely to have children), mail people only of a certain income level, or use other variables to target specifically who receives your mailing. By sending mail to just those households that are more likely to be receptive to your message, you will save money by not sending mail to those who are not of your target audience.

### Personas

It's easy to fall into stereotypes and embrace general assumptions about users when discussing target groups. Personas are a helpful tool that can help you be specific about user groups' needs and interests. Alison Martin and Helen Black write: "Creating a persona is about creating a language that everyone in your organization can understand and use effectively when talking about who the audience groups are."[9] A persona is a bit of shorthand to remind you and your colleagues that Kaede (an online-only, nontraditional student) has different needs than Fareed (a recent high school graduate). When you're discussing new marketing ideas, personas make it easier to think about Fareed's potential interests and where he'll consume media.

The best personas are based upon interviews with actual users of your organization. Each persona is a fictional characterization of the interests, needs, challenges, and opportunities for a target audience. They're not a write-up of a single, real person within that group. You can combine personas with other techniques to develop the most robust understanding of your users.

### Resources

- Usability.gov, "Personas," https://www.usability.gov/how-to-and-tools/methods/personas.html
- Shlomo "Mo" Goltz, "A Closer Look at Personas: What They Are and How They Work," 2014, https://www.smashingmagazine.com/2014/08/a-closer-look-at-personas-part-1

- National Archives, "Digital Personas," https://www.archives.gov/digital strategy/personas
- Tim Noetzel, "How to Improve Your Design Process with Data-Based Personas," 2018, https://www.smashingmagazine.com/2018/04/ design-process-data-based-personas

## NOTES

1. American Library Association, "Professional Ethics," 2008, www.ala.org/tools/ ethics.

2. Society of American Archivists, "SAA Core Values Statement and Code of Ethics," 2012, https://www2.archivists.org/statements/saa-core-values-statement-and -code-of-ethics.

3. American Alliance of Museums, "AAM Code of Ethics for Museums," 2000, http:// aam-us.org/resources/ethics-standards-and-best-practices/code-of-ethics.

4. EUR-Lex, 2016, http://data.europa.eu/eli/reg/2016/679/oj.

5. U.S. Census Bureau, "List of All Surveys," https://www.census.gov/programs -surveys/are-you-in-a-survey/survey-list.html.

6. Google, "About Fusion Tables," https://support.google.com/fusiontables/answer/ 2571232.

7. Tableau Public, "Preventing Workbook Downloads on Tableau Public," 2018, https://kb.tableau.com/articles/howto/preventing-workbook-downloads.

8. Claritas, "MyBestSegments," https://claritas360.claritas.com/mybestsegments.

9. Alison Martin and Helen Black, "Doing Less, Better: Targeting Audiences Effectively through Personas," 2011, www.culturehive.co.uk/resources/using -personas-to-target-audiences-more-effectively.

*chapter* 8

# Tracking and Reports

IF YOU LIKE DATA, COMPILING REPORTS IS PROBABLY A FAVORITE PART OF your job. In reports you get to see if your efforts are paying off, look for new opportunities, and share what you have learned. The guides in this chapter will steer you through questions that can be answered by tracking your work, the reports you can compile throughout the year from this data, how to run A/B tests to find the best way to promote your materials, and how to capture data through URL shorteners. The data you collect for each time period can then be compiled into reports that you can share with others.

This chapter is organized by the data you should be checking on within a particular time frame. (Your organization's interests and reporting schedules may differ.) In general, you will want to gather any data that is useful. Your best option is to gather data automatically without any manual oversight. That way you can look back for trends over time even if you don't know what you may want to look at in the future (Guide 48: "Questions to Ask").

Please note that I am not a statistician, so this guide highlights the kinds of insights you may be able to pull from different data sources. The questions below are examples of things you can try to learn from the data you collect. Then you can answer the questions within your reports and share them with others.

## GUIDE 48: Questions to Ask

### INDIVIDUAL CAMPAIGN
- For A/B-tested subject lines on your e-mails, which subject lines received the most opens (Guide 57: "A/B Testing")?

- Were there more clicks by users who received one subject line vs. another?
- Where did they click in the e-mail? Button, link, or image?
- Did word choices influence users' engagement (e.g., Buy Tickets vs. Purchase Tickets)?
- Once a link was clicked, did the users follow through on the website (e.g., by buying tickets)?
- For the web page that is linked, how many people left the website without going to another page? (This is called the "bounce rate.")

## YEARLONG CAMPAIGN
- What were your numbers at the beginning?
- What were your numbers at the end?
- What were your goals?
- Did you increase or decrease the numbers related to your goal (e.g., increase attendance)?
- Who was your target audience? (Chapter 7: "Who Are Your Users?")
    - How were they targeted?
    - How did different demographics react?

- Which publicity methods were the most successful (e.g., newspaper ad vs. social media ad)?
- If the campaign marketed several things together (e.g., museum passes), which of those items did the best over this year?
- Did the seasons and general weather affect use (e.g., snow in the winter may lower attendance)?
- What are your goals for next year?
- What will you do differently in the year to come?

## E-MAIL NEWSLETTERS
- Opens
- Clicks
- Unsubscribes

    - Why did they unsubscribe?
    - Did users stay subscribed over the long term?
    - Are certain segments more likely to unsubscribe than others?
    - How many e-mails can I send without increasing unsubscribes?
- What is the best time/day to send e-mails?
- How many e-mail groups are they subscribed to?
- Did holidays (religious, cultural, government) affect open and click rates?

    - If yes, by how much?
- Were there global events that caused a decrease in engagement?

    - For example, national tragedies
- Which subject lines appeal the most: ones that are straight to the point (This Week at . . . ) or that are eye-catching (You're Invited or You Will Not Believe . . . )?

- How can I use A/B tests to get the most opens and engagements?
- Did a new design or layout change clicks or increase unsubscribes?
- What are your goals for next year?
- What will you do differently in the year to come?

## SOCIAL MEDIA
- What did you hope to achieve?
  - Increased followers, likes, engagements
  - Raise awareness—if so, how did you measure it?
- How did the posted types of content (photo, video, text, audio, poll) perform?
- Was there any large number of unsubscribes/unfollows? If so, what happened around then?
- Were there global events that caused a decrease in engagement?
  - For example, national tragedies
- Are there any new features of the social media platform that you can start to use?
- What are your goals for next year?
- What will you do differently in the year to come?
- Are there any social media platforms you can retire from?

## PRINTED MATERIALS
- Where did people find your printed material?
  - You can use unique custom URLs to see where your information was found (Guide 56: "Shortened URLs").
  - You can add custom URLs in ads, posters, postcards, bookmarks, and so on.
- Do certain sizes of materials get picked up more often than others?
- By doing an observational study in which you watch an area where a sign is posted, how often are people drawn to look at it?
- If you add a new printed item to your marketing materials, was there a noticeable uptick in new users, foot traffic, purchases, and so on?
  - If so, you should be careful not to correlate all new success to that additional venue. Watch it over several cycles.
- Try out a variety of design styles and colors, and see how they appeal to different audiences.

## VIDEOS
- How many new subscribers did you gain over a given time period?
- What were people commenting on?
  - Do I want more comments?
  - Are the contents of the comments something meaningful to me?

- How many likes, shares, and views did you gain over a given time period?
- Which types of video are most successful (e.g., fads, educational, fun)?
- How did the same video shared on more than one platform do in those areas?
- Can you do A/B testing on your videos?
    - Make them shorter.
    - Add or remove title bumpers.
    - Put titles directly over the picture and not over a solid-color bumper.
- What keywords perform the best?

## GUIDE 49: What to Track When

In the following pages, there is a lot of information about the different kinds of data you will be tracking and the types of reports you can generate in your work. Use this cheat sheet (below) to remind you of the data you should be looking at and whom to share your reports with that you create from that data.

### DAILY
- Social media and e-mail newsletters: Report to your supervisor if you receive really good or bad feedback on these.

### WEEKLY
- Social media, newspaper, and online mentions of your organization: Report to all staff (if allowed) (Guide 58: "Marketing Report for Staff").

### MONTHLY
- Review sites, social media: Highlight the most interesting bits in the next weekly all-staff e-mail.
- Social media: Report to your supervisor and to social media creators.

### QUARTERLY
- E-mail newsletters: Report to your supervisor and other interested parties.
- Social media: Report to your supervisor and to social media creators.
- Year-round campaigns: Report to your colleague on the project, and your supervisor.

### ANNUALLY
- Annual report: Send to your supervisor.
- Staff wish-list review: Report to individual departments.

### SINGLE CAMPAIGNS
- Report to the person you worked with in developing the marketing plan.

# GUIDE 50: Daily Tracking and Reports

This guide covers the areas of your work you should check every day. If you do not stay on top of these areas you could run into challenges like negative comments on social media that are not addressed in a timely fashion. Or you could miss opportunities to fulfill publicity requests from local news organizations.

## E-MAILS

Checking your e-mails is a task that you are likely doing every day anyway. Your users should have a way to e-mail people at your organization, so be sure your e-mail address is given in the appropriate locations. As the marketing person, you want potential partners and feedback to come to you, so be sure your e-mail address is listed on all of your press releases, e-mail newsletters, and on the website (Guide 62: "Press Releases").

It is also helpful to turn on notifications from social media platforms. Tweak the settings so you are only getting e-mail notifications of new messages or comments, not likes or shares. If someone starts complaining on social media over the weekend, you want to know about it sooner rather than whenever you get around to checking that account on Monday.

Here is a tip that may not suit your organization: If you are the head of all social media and e-mail newsletters, consider peeking at your work e-mail a few times over the weekend and on holidays. This also allows you to catch any social media disasters before they can blow up for two days while you are at home. If this is not something that works for your organization, establish who will keep an eye on the social media accounts at night and on the weekends.

## SOCIAL MEDIA

If you can swing it, set up a second monitor at your desk to keep social media streams on. Free options include Tweetdeck (https://tweetdeck.twitter.com/), which only allows Twitter management, while Hootsuite (https://hootsuite.com/) supports a variety of social media networks. You don't need to watch the feeds all day but glancing at them a few times an hour gives you opportunities to react in almost real time to users' comments.

Some suggested feeds to set up on Tweetdeck:

- Users that your organization follows
- Comments directed at your organization (i.e., NeverlandArchives)
- A custom search for mentions of your organization (e.g., Neverland Archives)
- Your organization's direct messages (DMs)

If there is a hashtag that is used locally (e.g., #NameofTown), you may want a feed dedicated to that hashtag. That way, you can keep up with local area tweets or posts on other social media accounts (e.g., Instagram can cross-post to Twitter). For other social media tips, see Guide 71: "Social Media Tips."

Note: Check on Facebook every day for any notifications. This should only take a couple minutes. You should only do the deeper dive once a week (Guide 51: "Weekly Tracking and Reports").

For help with scheduling or understanding your networks, look for social media management software. One popular option is Buffer (https://buffer.com/). Check the G2 Crowd website for crowd-sourced verified reviews for other software options. It also offers tools to help you select which social media management tool is right for you.[1]

Beware of posting the exact same post on all networks. For example, Pinterest is popular with women and crafters. Consider posting your retirement planning event on Facebook instead. Or adjust your post slightly so that it appeals to the audience of that platform.

## INGEST FORM

If you have set up an ingest form to collect marketing requests from your colleagues, check this daily for updates (Guide 7: "Ingest Form Setup"). The easiest way to manage this is to have e-mail notifications sent to you for each form that is submitted. If you can, read over each request the day it comes in, and then put it into your project management software to schedule out the tasks (Chapter 4: "Set Up Project Management").

## GUIDE 51: Weekly Tracking and Reports

Looking at your work on a week-by-week case allows you to look for patterns in the short term. This gives you time to react and make adjustments on a timelier basis than if you were looking at the data only once a quarter. This section highlights what you should be tracking on a weekly basis as well as what to share in your weekly report with others.

### E-MAIL NEWSLETTERS

If you are sending weekly e-mails out, write a report at least four days after the e-mail went out on the effectiveness of the campaign. The report should only go to those who would find it to be of interest. A weekly e-mail focused on the organization's events then would be sent to those responsible for the events contained therein. You can offer to add others in your organization to your weekly e-mail, but ask before doing so, since this e-mail goes out so often. Keep this e-mail readable by using headers and bullet points to make it easy to scan.

### Overview

In your report, write a summary overview of how the campaign was received. This includes opens, click rate, unsubscribe rate and reasons given, and if you're doing A/B tests, what the variables were and what won (Guide 57: "A/B Testing"). I recommend not giving exact numbers on opens and clicks; instead, just compare them to the previous few weeks. Did they go up or down? Any guesses as to why (e.g., holidays)? This section should only be a paragraph long.

### Event Clicks

If this e-mail is for events, select the top 5 to 10 most-clicked-upon links to share. In a bullet list, write how many clicks there were and the name of the event. If this was a featured event, note that. If an event was registered, try to check the list of registrations. How many people signed up since the e-mail went out? If those e-mail clicks don't turn into registrations, ask yourself why this is so. Was there an obstacle preventing registration? Did something major happen in the news that might draw people elsewhere that day? At best, you are making educated guesses to help you understand your users' interests based upon their clicks.

It is helpful to share the most clicked-upon event so the number of clicks can be matched with in-person attendance. Did events highlighted in an e-mail bring more people to the event? This tactic is not a foolproof indicator of users' interest. However, if the e-mail clicks reliably match high in-person attendance, it could help your program's sponsors plan more efficiently for the event. Will they need to get more chairs?

If you wanted to go the extra mile, you could keep a spreadsheet that notes the most popular event clicks in each week's e-mail. Then get the number of attendees for those programs to add in. Over time, you may discover patterns.

Note: If you put all the information about the event in the e-mail, why should they click through to your website? A best practice for many audiences is to just put a teaser in the e-mail. Send them to your website, where they may then also look at other resources and services.

### Social Media Clicks

Most e-mail newsletters should contain links to your social media accounts. Add a line of text above the social media links/icons to invite users to follow you. Or tell them what you do on a particular account (e.g., you tweet new resources on Twitter). By tracking these clicks, it tells you a bit about what social media accounts your e-mail newsletter followers are using already.

### NEWSPAPERS AND THE WEB

The e-mail newsletter information is targeted at a very specific audience of colleagues. The following topics are to help you create a weekly report. You can leave out the e-mail newsletter information for this report. I gather the following information, links, and screencaps and paste them into an e-mail to share with staff (Guide 58: "Marketing Report for Staff"). You can also capture this in word-processing software and share it within your department.

### Newspaper and Online Mentions

This task may become difficult or impossible to stay up on if your community has daily newspapers. In that case, just do a web search for "your institution name" and set the search parameters for the past week. Make sure to click past the first page of results to look for all instances. You will likely discover many spam websites that include your organization's name. Ignore them.

Instead, look for news articles, blog posts, reviews, and write-ups on your staff that mention where they work. Again, if in doubt with anything regarding the staff, ask them for permission to include them in your weekly report. They may not want everyone knowing they did a workshop. However, they may not mind you sharing that they wrote an article for a professional journal.

If you want to check a daily print newspaper, you can save time by only checking around the time your press releases may have been published (Guide 62: "Press Releases"). Ask your colleagues to alert you if a reporter shows up unexpectedly to photograph events. News outlets tend to be interested in national trending stories (e.g., a solar eclipse), controversy (e.g., book challenges), community-wide kid events (e.g., Summer Reading), and big name visitors to your organization.

You can track these news and online mentions in a spreadsheet (which is useful if connecting them to press releases), in a knowledge base (Guide 13: "Personal Knowledge Base"), or in a weekly report to your colleagues (Guide 58: "Marketing Report for Staff").

### Facebook Interactivity

Facebook will change its algorithm many times before you read this text. So the best advice here is to go into your account and check the Insights tab (you will need a business account). Click around on the various options and see what you can learn about your audience, how popular your content is, and who is interacting with your organization. Depending on the metrics that are of most interest to you, you can check to see how your followers are reacting to your content. As of early 2018, Facebook is showing only a tiny percentage of followers any content from any page they follow. This is so Facebook can encourage more ad buys.

Here are some suggested items to check each week:

- Which posts were the most popular?
- Did your content receive any comments, shares, mentions, or was tagged in anything? You should notice things that need a response during your daily check-in.
- Which posts resulted in unsubscribes?
- Did anyone sign up to attend an event?

As of this writing, Facebook uses green and red to indicate how your stats are doing. These numbers can look alarming. If you ran an ad one week and not the next, the week after the ad runs may show a dramatic decrease in views or new followers. Don't let this spook you. Instead, focus on big leaps in engagement and follows. What did you do in the past week that may have caused that?

*Social Media*

You should capture screenshots and links to community engagements with your social media channels. These posts let you demonstrate how the community feels about your organization. Sometimes you even get charming interactions that can go into a report to the board.

You should exercise discretion if a staff member tags your organization or interacts with your post. You may want to ask the staffer directly whether they mind if you include them in your weekly report. They may not realize that by selecting a location for their social media post you can also see it because it tagged the organization. For example, if a staff member's child came to a library event, the staffer may have posted a photo online and tagged the library. They may not want all their colleagues to know about that post. Ask whenever you are in doubt.

When working on your report, look beyond just direct interactions with followers (e.g., they tagged you). Check hashtags and location tags as well.

## GUIDE 52: Monthly Tracking and Reports

For monthly tracking and reports, there are two main areas you should check: review sites and the number of social media followers you have on different platforms. These data sources usually do not need to be checked more than once a month.

### REVIEW SITES

Search engines may pull reviews from established venue rating sites to rate your organization. Google uses its own rating system, while Bing uses TripAdvisor.com. Sign your organization up for an account at each of the major sites. Then claim your organization's location. You will have opportunities to upload photos and fill out information, and you can be alerted to new comments or ratings. Include the positive ratings in your weekly staff report (Guide 58: "Marketing Report for Staff").

You may want to set an e-mail alert for new comments on rating sites. If something negative is said, your organization will need to quickly decide how to respond (or not). Check Guide 67: "Handling Complaints" for tips on how to handle negative commentary.

### SOCIAL MEDIA

Aside from keeping abreast of social media on a daily and weekly basis, you should capture your stats every month. Which numbers are important to your organization will vary, but followers is an important one. Some platforms make it difficult to see how many followers you had on a particular day, so schedule to track these sites on the same day each month (first or last).

To go a step further, compare your growth/decline of followers each month. If something is unexpectedly growing fast, you can note it in a weekly staff report as an interesting tidbit. Figure 8.1 gives a simple example of this comparison chart.

### How to Compare Monthly Social Media Stats

1. Visit each site you have an account on and write down your key numbers.
   - Social media sites
   - Google My Business (Guide 66: "Google My Business")
2. Pull up the previous month's numbers.
   - I store this information in my project management system as a recurring monthly task.
3. Use your calculator or a site like Percentage Calculator (https://percentage calculator.net) to find out the percentage increase/decrease.
4. Write the calculated number down.
   - I round up to the first digit. It is important to be consistent in how you round numbers; for example, 1.75% becomes 1.8%.
5. Positive numbers indicate growth, while negative numbers show a loss. If numbers go up or down in a big way, write down some guesses as to the causes.
6. Share this report with your supervisor and anyone else who may be interested. Figure 8.1 is an example.

|           | April 2020 | May 2020 | Difference |
|-----------|------------|----------|------------|
| Facebook  | 1286       | 1284     | -0.2%      |
| Instagram | 1617       | 1909     | 18.1%      |
| Twitter   | 1345       | 1361     | 1.2%       |

**FIGURE 8.1**
**Example of a month-to-month chart comparing social media stats**

## GUIDE 53: Quarterly Tracking and Reports

Quarterly reports are the main ones I send out to colleagues. They cover a time period that is in recent memory, but which provides enough data to show significant changes. Since you will be compiling so many quarterly reports, consider only sending these reports to staff whose work can be seen in the report. So send the social media report to your supervisor and the other people who handle social media, not to every department head.

### E-MAIL NEWSLETTERS

Every quarter, enter into a spreadsheet the numbers that matter to your organization from your e-mail newsletters. Your fields will differ, but this gives you an overall picture of how engagement with your newsletter audience changes over the course of the year. Then you can use that in your annual tracking (Guide 54: "Annual Tracking and Reports").

This task can take two hours per recurring e-mail newsletter list. You may want to focus your attention on only one list instead of trying to track each list. For example, the weekly/monthly events newsletter vs. teen-only e-mails.

### How to Set Up a Quarterly Spreadsheet

The example below is for a weekly events e-mail. See Guide 27: "E-Mail Newsletters" for information on e-mail newsletter concepts.

1. In your spreadsheet, create a new worksheet and add in your column titles across the top.
   - Date, Segment, Opens, Clicks, Subject Line, Teaser Text, Featured Event, Unsub(scribes), Bounces, Unsub Reason, Notes
2. Name this sheet _Template. Then duplicate it for this quarter.
3. Name your new sheet by year and then month range; for example, 2022 Jan. to Mar.
4. Fill in your rows to match your columns. For Notes, this is for anything that may be helpful to know (e.g., the town lost power, there was a holiday weekend, or you changed your e-mail design).
5. At the bottom of the Open, Clicks, Unsub, and Bounce columns, add your totals.
   - Try to use a formula to automate the calculations.
   - Check your software to see how to quickly select all items in a column.
6. Somewhere else on your spreadsheet, set up a small table to capture your average rates.
7. You can copy and paste this easily into an annual spreadsheet.
8. Use background colors to make your table easier to read and scan the most important data at a glance.
9. You may be able to copy and paste your tables right into e-mails or a word processor to make a shareable quarterly report.
10. Next quarter, duplicate the template tab and rename it to the appropriate date range.

### Other Tables to Consider

*Compare to Previous Years.* Compare this quarter to the same time period in previous years. Make sure to keep an eye on factors that would cause a change to the numbers. For example, the frequency of how often an e-mail goes out, new e-mail designs, segmenting your audiences, or changing e-mail newsletter providers.

*Special Tests.* If you have done any special tests (especially A/B ones), make a table to capture that information. Include your average numbers (control) in one column/row and then your test averages next to/below the control. You can lay this out in whatever way makes sense to you. Add a Results cell to note the difference. If there is barely any change, you can use a phrase like "No difference." It may be helpful to add a note as to why you were testing this information. Figure 8.2 compares average open rates for two different subject lines during a twelve-week period. The results suggest that the straightforward subject line was more effective.

| Subject line | Average open rate |
| --- | --- |
| Discoveries at the archives this week | 36.4% |
| Funny or unusual | 27.5% |

**FIGURE 8.2**
**Examples of an A/B testing results table comparing subject lines**

*Audience Segmentation.* If you are using audience segmentation, you can compare the groups against each other in opens and clicks. Likewise, you can compare a segment against itself. How many subscribers did you have at the beginning of the quarter vs. the end? You can use absolute numbers here and represent them as percentages.

*Subject Line Tests.* If you are using A/B testing, you can compare the number of opens between the different types of subject lines you are testing (Guide 57: "A/B Testing"). Some categories of subject lines are:

- Asks a question
- Clickbait (e.g., "You will not believe how many people did this!")
- Formal/serious
- Funny
- How-to
- List (e.g., "Top 5 reasons to . . .")
- Negative (e.g., "Don't miss out")
- Number (e.g., "50% of users do this thing")
- Straight to the point (e.g., This Week at [Your Organization])

Note: Negative words, headlines, and ads get more clicks/opens than positive ones.[2]

*Uncovering Unsubscribes.* If you have a single featured event, did unsubscribe rates go up or down for different audiences? For instance, let's say you send out a weekly e-mail that includes programs for adults, teens, and kids. If most of your audience is not interested in teen events, do unsubscribes grow whenever a teen event is featured?

Be careful in how you communicate this test to your staff. Emphasize that you are not saying that you want to drop all teen events from the e-mail. Instead, you want it to be noted that you expect an increase in unsubscribes whenever those events are highlighted. Or the head of teens should not feel discouraged that teen events are not clicked upon in the e-mail. This e-mail's audience is not the same as their target one.

You can use these test results to argue for not featuring types of events that are a documented driver of unsubscribes.

*Number of Events.* If you have a slow time of year (e.g., summer) when you know your users may be out of town, your organization may host fewer events. Your audience may correspondingly open fewer e-mails or click less in them, since they have picked up on the fact that there is not much going on at your organization for them. If you wanted to pull a test out of this, you could compare the number of event types per e-mail (e.g., adult, teen, and child) over different times of the year to see if there are any patterns.

### Writing Your Quarterly Report

Your numbers are likely more fascinating to you than to your colleagues who will skim your report. Pull out the most important data, any information about test results, and suggested changes. You should write some context in order to help make sense of the numbers. Make sure to add in any visuals you create, even if it is just the tables.

Include yourself as a contact for your report e-mails. Then move the e-mail into a Reports or Stats e-mail folder. This will help you later find your report a little more easily.

Double-check your work before you send it. Percentage differences can be understood in two ways:

- Absolute Difference: The change between two numbers is noted as a subtraction.
- Relative Difference: The change is noted as a ratio.

What this means is that when you look at your overall e-mail opens for the year, the number may be 28 percent. The previous year it was 31.9 percent. With the simple subtraction of absolute difference, it looks like there was only a 3.9 percent drop in opens this year. However, if you compare the numbers as a ratio, you see that the true drop was − 12.3 percent. The relative difference is usually the number that makes an impression on the report's readers.

For a review of the technical differences between the two ways, check out the American College of Physicians' "Primer on Absolute vs. Relative Differences."[3]

### SOCIAL MEDIA

Repeat the work you did in your monthly social media tracking (Guide 52: "Monthly Tracking and Reports"). The real value of this quarterly report will be when you have at least one quarter to look back upon. Since the quarter is recent, compile notes of big events (e.g., programs, weather, holidays, marketing pushes, paid ads) that could have affected the growth or decline of your numbers.

If you were less active on a social media platform during the quarter, note that. Your engagement numbers will be down if you have not been posting.

## YEAR-ROUND CAMPAIGNS

Once you settle into your marketing position, you may team up with colleagues to create year-round promotional campaigns. So to help you make adjustments in your strategy, you will need to check in every quarter on how you are doing.

Depending on your strategy, you may be reporting back on:

- Attendance/resource use
- E-mail opens and clicks
- Registration
- Social media engagement
- Website clicks

## GUIDE 54: Annual Tracking and Reports

For the long-term picture, you will track your stats over the year and create a big annual snapshot of your work. I suggest not going into too much detail since you can refer people back to the previous reports (especially monthly) if they want to learn more about the factors that influenced the numbers throughout the year. You will then round out year-end activities by checking back in with your colleagues about how their needs have changed in the past twelve months.

## E-MAIL NEWSLETTERS

For simplicity's sake, the annual report I will describe here focuses on only one e-mail newsletter. The year of this newsletter is from January to December. You may need to do a fiscal-year report instead, which starts and ends during other times of the year. This particular example covers a report that includes several years' worth of data split over quarters. Figure 8.3 is a six-month comparison of e-mail opens and clicks over the course of three years.

1. Return to your quarterly e-mail newsletter reports, each of which should be one spreadsheet with multiple worksheets/tabs (Guide 53: "Quarterly Tracking and Reports"). Your data will come from these worksheets.

2. Create a new worksheet within this spreadsheet and title it *20XX Year in Review*.

3. Create a table to compare opens and clicks throughout the year.

   a. In the first row, title your chart *20XX Opens and Clicks*.

   b. In the second row, enter *Jan to Mar Comparisons*.

   c. Starting in the second column, create these three table headings: *Year, Open, Clicks*.

   d. Copy those three headings. Place your mouse in the empty cell next to *Clicks*. Paste in your headings. Repeat this twice more. Now you have four quarters' worth of data.

   e. In the cell under the first *Year*, put the year that just passed. Enter that year's data across the row.

   f. These opens and clicks are the average for that quarter.

| | January to March Comparisons | | | April to June Comparisons | | | Total Average Opens per Year | Total Average Clicks per Year |
|---|---|---|---|---|---|---|---|---|
| | Year | Opens | Clicks | Year | Opens | Clicks | | |
| | 2019 | 36.5 | 6.4 | 2019 | 36.2 | 6.3 | 36.4 | 6.4 |
| | 2018 | 21.8 | 3.2 | 2018 | 25.1 | 5.1 | 21.5 | 4.2 |
| | 2017 | 21.6 | 2.1 | 2017 | 21.3 | 4.8 | 21.5 | 3.4 |
| Averages | | 26.6 | 3.9 | | 27.5 | 5.4 | 26.5 | 4.7 |

FIGURE 8.3
Example of a six-month review of e-mail statistics

    g. In the next row down, put in the year before that. Repeat as far back as you have information or as of interest to you.

    h. In the first column, one row below your last year's information added, write *Averages*.

    i. Under each *Open* and *Clicks* column, average out the numbers.

4. Next to the final *Clicks* column, enter these header titles across the row: *Total Opens per Year* and *Total Clicks per Year.*

    a. While before you went across and averaged out each quarter's opens and clicks across multiple years, this time you are looking at the numbers just for that year.

    b. You cannot just highlight every cell in that row to get the average.

    c. Average only on the cells that match the data you are looking at for that year (i.e., *Opens* or *Clicks*).

    d. There is still an overall *Averages* row that you can calculate across for these two new columns.

5. Look at your data by quarter and annually to look for patterns.

    a. Have you increased opens or clicks over time?

    b. If not, strategize how you can try to improve your numbers this upcoming year.

Other tables can be created using this method:

- If you segment this e-mail into smaller groups (e.g., *Old Subscribers, New Subscribers*), you can do a quarterly and annual comparison chart too.

    - Are New Subscribers more likely to open e-mails throughout the year?

    - Which time of year do Old Subscribers click e-mails the most?

- You can create a simple table to compare groups of years against each other. This works great if you have any big changes that could cause numbers to change:

    - You weeded out people who had not opened any e-mail in a year.

    - You drastically redesigned the e-mail.

    - You changed the frequency of e-mails.

## COMPARE YEARLY CAMPAIGNS

If you have programs or campaigns that repeat each year, you can compare the statistics from last year to this one (see "What Is Marketing?" in Chapter 1). To make this work, you need to gather stats for each of your major campaigns throughout the year.

Note: Individual annual campaign comparisons will be done at the end of this year's campaign. Don't save this for an end-of-year or start-of-year review. Do this review as each year's annual campaign finishes up. You want to get the data about how that big fund-raiser did to the organizers as soon as possible after the campaign finishes up—not at the end of your fiscal or calendar year.

1. Before the campaign repeats, look at last year's information to refresh yourself. Is there anything new you can add to last year's ideas? Are there any changes to make?
2. Once the campaign is over for the year, gather this year's data and check that data against the prior year (Guide 55: "Single Campaigns").
3. Compare this year's report to the previous one.
4. Look for patterns, changes in technology, and changes in users' behaviors or interests to help you plan to do better next year.
5. Share your findings with your colleague who ran the program or event.

## CHECK YOUR LIST

It's now time to revisit the wish list your colleagues shared with you when you started in this role (Guide 1: "Getting Staff Buy-In"). You captured this information in a document. What were you able to do this past year? What proved insurmountable? Is there a better way to do something now? Write these notes on your document. Highlight in red any outstanding items that you still need to do. Then turn to your calendar and start planning out when you will address these concerns.

Then create a document to share with each department. Share only what is public-friendly knowledge (i.e., not their tips on how to handle a difficult colleague) in this document. Include only the information from this department. If there are things you still need to do, share when you plan to work on that item.

## CHECK IN WITH COLLEAGUES

You should schedule time to meet again with your colleagues to ask how your marketing went for them this past year. What would make their lives easier now? Do they have any ideas that they would like to try? This session is much more casual than your initial data-gathering meeting. Ideally, you should have this conversation before you need to submit next year's budget requests. That way, if someone suggests something you'd really like to try, you can ask for funding to make it possible.

You can also use this time to ask about your colleagues' plans for the coming year. You should find out about new programs, services, staff changes, and goals. Take time to consider how your work plays into their overall plans, and share that with them after you have had time to process it. Consider waiting until you have talked to everyone, so you have an overarching view of the organization's plans for the coming year.

## CHECK IN WITH SUPERVISOR

This past year you have done a lot of work and gathered a lot of data. Perhaps you have been able to keep your supervisor informed on your work through your regularly scheduled meetings. Even if you have, put together a list of your top accomplishments, how your ideas made a difference, and suggest changes for the coming year. If you have this conversation after the one with your colleagues, you can impress your boss by showing that you understand the big picture.

## GUIDE 55: Single Campaigns

Unlike the previous guides in this chapter, this guide details how to write a report for a single campaign (see "What Is Marketing?" in Chapter 1).

## YOUR GOAL

Are you going to spend a lot of effort to promote a single event or promotion? Are you creating many promotional items (e.g., bookmarks, e-mail announcement, flyers, social media, etc.) for this campaign? Then you want to write a report afterwards to measure how your marketing efforts helped this campaign succeed.

**DIFFICULTY LEVEL** Intermediate.

**TIME** 60 to 90 minutes.

**COST** Free.

## WHAT YOU NEED TO START

Since this campaign was a major effort, you should have a publicity plan that lists most of your marketing efforts (Guide 15: "Publicity Plans"). As you created your weekly (Guide 51: "Weekly Tracking and Reports") and monthly (Guide 52: "Monthly Tracking and Reports") reports, you should have captured information as you went along about mentions of the campaign in various outlets like the newspaper.

## TOOLS

- Publicity plan
- Previous reports
- Internet access
- E-mail
- Log-in access to gather analytics data

**WHAT YOU NEED TO KNOW**

At this point, most of your work has already been done. You are just gathering all the data into one place now to share with your colleagues. A more complex version of this report can be found in Guide 14: "Internal Tracking System."

**STEPS**

1. Complete the items from your publicity plan (Guide 15: "Publicity Plans").
2. Use well-formed UTM links to help you track your numbers in your analytics software (Guide 56: "Shortened URLs").
3. Add a reminder to your calendar to ask the person in charge of the event for their numbers afterwards:
   a. Attendance registration
   b. Actual head count
4. In a mini-report to your colleague, go through each of your marketing plan's items to gather the stats from it:
   a. E-mail opens and clicks
   b. Social media clicks, likes, replies
   c. Event registration via social media
   d. Website page hits and clicks
   e. Newspaper and online mentions
   f. Use numbers (if a service)
5. Analyze the data you have gathered by noting what worked, what did not, and your ideas for next time.
6. Save your report in your internal tracking system for next year (Guide 14: "Internal Tracking System").
7. Share your report with your colleague who is responsible for the program, event, or service. An e-mail works well for this.

**TIPS**

If this campaign repeats annually, start preparing for next year by checking the annual tracking list (Guide 54: "Annual Tracking and Reports"). You should consider creating a spreadsheet to track how the major repeating campaigns like fund-raising events do each year.

Did the local newspapers run less coverage of a repeating event or campaign this year than usual? Try to figure out any factors that may have influenced their decision. Perhaps too much else was going on this year. Or they now consider your campaign's press release to be an attempt at an unpaid ad. If you really cannot guess as to the reason, consult with your supervisor and director. Maybe something else is going on. If you have a mutually beneficial, great relationship with a news outlet, you might reach out and ask them directly for insight on how you can change your strategy for next year. Be careful, though, if the relationship is in any way sensitive.

**WATCH OUT!**
You may have done a lot of work to promote an event that fell flat. This is outside of your control. Sometimes an event or promotion simply does not resonate with your audience.

Your colleagues may not be interested in a carefully prepared report. Before you do all this work, ask them if they would like the report. Ask if it would be useful to them. If they say no, spend your time elsewhere. The only single campaign reports I would consider doing even if staff are not interested are major fund-raisers.

## GUIDE 56: Shortened URLs

**YOUR GOAL**
Is anyone clicking on your links? Did you know that by default, Google Analytics does not track links which go off your website? You can pick up great insights about your community's interests by using shortened URLs. If you have ever copied a 200-character URL into a chat window or e-mail, you know how painful it looks. You can clean this up by using URL shorteners instead and change those long URLs to short ones that pack a double whammy: they can be used for branding purposes *and* to track link clicks.

**DIFFICULTY LEVEL** Varies from easy to intermediate.

**TIME** Varies.

**COST** Free or low cost.

**WHAT YOU NEED TO START**
Get the all-clear from your supervisor to start using a link shortening/tracking service. Your organization may have privacy concerns.

**TOOLS**
   • An account on Bitly.com
   • Consider a browser extension

**WHAT YOU NEED TO KNOW**
Bitly (https://bitly.com) is easy, fast, and free for most users. They provide charts that look impressive in your reports. Enterprise accounts give you much greater flexibility, reports, and tools to understand your data. However, the cost is hundreds of dollars per month.

## STEPS

### Beginner Steps

1. Create a Bitly.com account so you can start tracking your links at Bitly.com.
2. You can immediately start creating bitlinks (their name for shortened URLs) by just copying and pasting your URLs into the service.
3. Bitlinks can be tagged to help you organize them. Check the discussion of tags below in the "Tips" section for guidance.
4. Copy the link into your social media, your e-mail newsletters, your website's links to external sites, and signage.
   - If you are using the default bit.ly/1xixKW, you can customize the text behind the forward slash.
   - If you have a custom domain and a free account, you cannot customize the end of the URL as of this publication.
5. Visit Bitly.com to see stats about how your links are performing. If you use a link for a long period, you can see when it gets more clicked-upon over time.
   - The life cycle of how long a link is clicked upon is very short. In my experience, the first twenty-four hours is the most active time.
6. Within Bitly.com, there are filters to look at your stats by tag.
   - This is a quick way to see which types of content in a monthly e-mail perform over time.
7. Bitlinks can be searched. It can be hit or miss whether it will pull the right full-length URL from within your profile, though.
8. If you want to see how your link is doing without logging in, just add a plus sign to the end of the URL. This trick works with everyone's bitlinks. It doesn't provide full information, but it shows a bit of data.

### Advanced Steps

1. If you are using Google Analytics (GA), you will need to modify your bitlinks so that GA can track them within their dashboard.
2. Use the Google Campaign URL Builder (https://ga-dev-tools.appspot.com/campaign-url-builder). See figure 8.4.
   a. This extra code is an Urchin Tracking Module (UTM) which adds extra parameters to a link so it can be tracked.
   b. We will be filling out the form as shown in figure 8.4.
3. Fill out the fields listed below, at a minimum. Use underscores between words within a single field.
   a. Website URL: This is the original URL from a website, not the bitlink one.
   b. Campaign Source: Where will you post this link (e.g., in an announcement e-mail)? Then write *20250201_announcement.*

| | |
|---|---|
| * **Website URL** | https://www.bestmuseumever.org/minigolf |

The full website URL (e.g. `https://www.example.com` )

| | |
|---|---|
| * **Campaign Source** | single_event_2020-10-10 |

The referrer: (e.g. `google` , `newsletter` )

| | |
|---|---|
| **Campaign Medium** | email |

Marketing medium: (e.g. `cpc` , `banner` , `email` )

| | |
|---|---|
| **Campaign Name** | 2020_minigolf |

Product, promo code, or slogan (e.g. `spring_sale` )

| | |
|---|---|
| **Campaign Term** | |

Identify the paid keywords

| | |
|---|---|
| **Campaign Content** | |

Use to differentiate ads

---

## Share the generated campaign URL

Use this URL in any promotional channels you want to be associated with this custom campaign

> https://www.bestmuseumever.org/minigolf?utm_source=single_event_2020-10-
> 10&utm_medium=email&utm_campaign=2020_minigolf

Set the campaign parameters in the fragment portion of the URL (not recommended).

🗖 Copy URL     ∞ Convert URL to Short Link (authorization required)

**FIGURE 8.4**
**Screenshot of Google Analytics' Campaign URL Builder**

c. Campaign Medium: Which platform are you posting this link on? Is it an e-mail, a paid ad, your website, social media (be specific which one), and so on?

d. Campaign Name: *This is the key field.* If you consistently use the same campaign name for a group of related links, you can then see them all under one name in Google Analytics.

    i. For example, let's link to your spring fund-raiser ticket page. Name your campaign *name 2025_spring fundraiser.*

    ii. Then, for every place you plan to post a link to the ticket page, you will want to use the *2025_spring fundraiser* campaign name.

    iii. In the *Campaign Source* and *Campaign Medium* fields, put in specifically where you are posting the link. You may want to include the date of your posting within the campaign source in order to help distinguish between the different days you tweeted the link out (e.g., *campaign source: 20250201_tweet*).

4. As you add text to the four fields, you will notice that the generated link at the bottom of the page gets longer. It will include every word you put in fields b through d. Since these terms will be visible to whomever clicks on the link, make sure they are something you wouldn't mind the public saying (e.g., "leads" vs. "newbies").

5. Copy the generated link over to Bitly.com to get the shortened URL. Make sure to add a tag.

6. Paste the link wherever it is intended to go.

7. Wait a while for your links to get some clicks before heading over to Google Analytics. Then navigate over to Acquisition > Campaigns > All Campaigns.

8. You should now see the campaign title that you used for all links related to the fund-raiser ticket page under the title of *2025_spring fundraiser.*

9. When you click on the campaign name, now comes the magic: you can see all the links that were created under the same campaign named together. It is now easy to see whether your website, an e-mail, or social media post got your fund-raiser page the most hits. Use that information to strategize for next year (e.g., try buying more ads).

## TIPS

Watch your local news' websites and social media accounts. If they are using Bitly links (bit.ly/somethinghere), you can use the + trick to see how many clicks their links receive. This broader net lets you see your community's interests outside of your immediate user base.

You can install the Bitly browser plug-in/extension on all staff computers that will use shortened URLs. This produces a little button in their browser which they can then click on to generate a bitlink right then and there.

You should create and enforce a controlled vocabulary of tags. Your life will be easier if everyone is using a single term like "Twitter" instead of "Tweet," "Tweets," "TW," and so on. The official Bitly Chrome extension's tag field is search-based and suggests previously used tags. The suggestions are fast, but this decreases accuracy for infrequent users to correctly tag links. The older Bitly extension showed a list of tags instead of searching for a preexisting tag. So be aware that infrequent users may not realize that you have a controlled vocabulary and tag a link "Tweet" instead of "Twitter."

Try to get everyone to tag all shortened links they share. This will help you filter bitlinks later on.

You should use abbreviations and acronyms with care. They should make obvious sense to most casual link taggers (e.g., FB is Facebook). Exceptions exist for organizations that are well-structured and track each of their tags closely. Then it may make sense to use more complicated naming structures.

Look for browser extensions that will help shorten your URLs and also automatically add them to a Google Sheet. The companies that do this change their names frequently or go out of business, so do a search for who offers that functionality right now.

**WATCH OUT!**
Bitly allows custom URL domain (my.lib/whatever) instead of Bitly links (bit.ly/whatever). However, once you get a custom domain on a nonprofit account, you can no longer choose the text that goes after the forward slash. So your links will always look like *my.lib/1inQz3* instead of *bit.ly/mycoolevent*. However, the benefit of using a custom domain like my.lib is great for branding purposes. If you're lucky enough to get a custom domain which is easy to identify as your organization, your shortened URLs will really stand out in a sea of bit.ly or tinyurl.com shortened links.

You cannot delete a bitlink. They may only be hidden from your view while logged into Bitly.com.[4]

Bitly makes money based on the clicks on your links. Most companies that help you shorten your URLs will have a similar scheme in place. Alternatives to Bitly for link-tracking include Google URL shortener (all information about link clicks is public) and YOURLS (https://yourls.org). YOURLS is open source and gives you complete control over your URL shortening. However, this means that your organization has to set it up and maintain it, and it may not be as easy to use as a more commercial solution like Bitly.

## GUIDE 57: A/B Testing

### WHAT IS A/B TESTING
If you need to discover what appeals the most to users, A/B testing is your new best friend. This method allows you to take two concepts (A and B), share them with your users, and then get results back as to which concept was more popular. You can then feel more confident in your marketing efforts because you have people-tested evidence that one concept is better than another. Testing your concepts can save you time and money. If design A drives more registrations than B, you will need to do less promotion, since your tickets will sell out faster.

A/B testing relies on having at least two versions (keep it simple and start with two) of a thing that you want to test. One may be a control, which is the way you have been doing things, while the other is the experiment. The most precise way to do A/B testing is to test only one item out at a time. For instance, if you want to design a better website home page, try changing the header text first, and then the color of a button. By testing one item at a time, you can eliminate concepts that don't drive the user to act in the desired way (e.g., clicking a link).

## WHAT TO TEST

You can test almost anything. A/B testing is easier when done digitally, but you can conduct it in the real world as well. The sections below are some broad areas that you can test. A test variable such as whether people prefer one color over another can be tested online (e.g., the color of a website button) or in the real world (e.g., the color of a bookmark).

### Digital via Clicks
- E-mail subject lines
- Content (buttons, links)
- Images
- Website layouts
- Navigation menus
- Colors
- Word choices

### Analog
- Displays and exhibits
- Signage
- Printed materials (e.g., posters, postcards)
- Furniture placement
- Questionnaires

## HOW TO TEST

There are many tools available to help you A/B test a concept. With digital methods, the software will show a random selection of your users either concept A or B. The design that gets the most interaction (usually clicks) will then be shown to the rest of your users. This method works well with e-mail, since the test is run and then the winning concept is delivered automatically to the rest of your mailing list. You can then be sure that you have given your best shot at achieving your objectives, since your design has been tested on actual users. The examples below give you an overview of how you can use A/B testing in your work.

### E-Mail

If you are designing an e-mail newsletter, you are likely creating it through a platform like MailChimp (https://mailchimp.com). Your platform may then allow you to A/B test elements like the subject line, sender name, content, or delivery time. The first two are straightforward, but you can get creative with what "testing content" means. It could be testing the text, layouts, colors, buttons, or images. You can test your text by using the person's name, changing the tone from formal to casual, shortening or lengthening sentences, or even changing font sizes.

### Website

Your website analytics software may offer A/B testing as well. Three popular options are Google Analytics (https://www.google.com/analytics/), Crazy Egg (https://crazyegg.com), and Kissmetrics (https://www.kissmetricshq.com). Of these three, Google Analytics is free. You will need to add their code to your website so the tests can be run.

In Google Analytics, you create two different website page designs, and then enter the URLs into your Analytics dashboard. Whenever someone goes to that page (e.g., your home page), they will be shown either the first or the second web page design. Your test runs as long as you specified. At the end, you can then look at the results and see the winning design.

### Displays

The type of displays your colleagues put together in your building will determine how this A/B test works out. You will likely need several people's full cooperation to help you, since this is not an automatic test like you can do online. Let's say that you have a display of printed materials that users are encouraged to take. Carefully count out how many copies of each item you are putting out. Then place them on the display. At the end of your time period (at least a week), count the remaining number of handouts of each type. The assistance of your colleagues comes into play here. If they notice that one item is running out and they must make more copies, they need to alert you to how many copies they are putting out so your final numbers are accurate.

A few things you can learn:

- Which items do better in this location?
- Which exhibit method gets more interaction: books lying flat on the table, in stacks, or standing up?
- Does adding decorative details help draw users' attention (e.g., a plain display vs. one with balloons)?

### Postcard

Put a different website address, phone number, or keyword (to enter onto a form) on each of your two test postcards. After a set period of time, see which one had a greater number of engagement from users. Then print more copies of the winning design to send out.

### Making Sense of the Results

There is a drawback to how great and easy it is to use A/B testing: sometimes the results don't show a strong preference either way. While this can be frustrating, it does mean that you can at least continue onwards with some guidance on which type is more appealing. A/B testing is an iterative process where you continuously keep testing in order to improve. This is easiest with e-mails, where you can test something every time you hit "send."

The preferred option's winning numbers will usually be small. However, if the open rate for design A is 4 percent while the rate for B is 12 percent, you can say that B's subject line received 3 times more opens. This looks great in your reports *and* helps you feel like there's a real difference going on here. If you are interested

in learning more about A/B testing, check out Jakub Linowski's "GoodUI Fastfor-
ward" website (https://goodui.org/patterns).

## GUIDE 58: Marketing Report for Staff

**YOUR GOAL**
As described in the tracking guide on weekly reports, you can create a report for
staff about how your community is interacting with the organization (Guide 51:
"Weekly Tracking and Reports").

**DIFFICULTY LEVEL** Intermediate.

**TIME** 1 to 2 hours per week.

**COST** Free.

**WHAT YOU NEED TO START**
Familiarize yourself with the tasks listed in the "Weekly Tracking and Reports"
guide.

**TOOLS**
- Local newspaper(s)
- E-mail, word processor
- Computer and browser
- Screen capture (likely built into your computer)

**WHAT YOU NEED TO KNOW**
This weekly report can quickly eat up your time. I started out with one hour per
week, but it sometimes takes two hours if things were particularly active on social
media that week. Try to stay within your time allotment.

**STEPS**
I started writing a weekly e-mail to department heads about mentions of our
library in newspapers, online, social media interactions, and the most popular
social media posts. Then I was encouraged to share this report with all staff each
week. Since then, I have been told: "I would never have known about this stuff if
it wasn't for your e-mail," "This is the only e-mail I read all the way through," and
"I look forward to reading this each week." The reception by staff was overwhelm-
ingly positive.

1. Open the information-capturing software of your choice (e-mail or word
   processor).

2. Create the big headers for information you will share:
   a. Newspapers and Online
   b. [Social Media Account I]
   c. [Social Media Account II]

3. As you go through each area described in the "Weekly Tracking and Reports" guide, look for interactions or mentions of your organization. Write a line to explain what you are capturing. Add a link to the mention within that descriptive text.
   a. Full sentences may not be needed.
   b. If a story unfolds over social media, share it. How did it start? Who was involved? What makes this a good tale?

4. Take a screenshot and then insert it into your e-mail or document. You may need to resize it.
   a. Screenshots may not be needed if there is no accompanying image. Sometimes just copying the comment is good enough.
   b. Include screenshots of photos that users tagged you in on social media. It's a sneak peek at what people love about your building and organization. You may discover that people appreciate your organization in ways you had no idea about!

5. For each social media platform, include your top post of the week.
   a. What were its stats (i.e., reach, impressions, likes, comments, shares)?
   b. Why do you think people reacted strongly to it with likes, comments, and/or shares?

**TIPS**

Depending on your institution, you may want to include only positive things in your e-mail. You should bring negative items to the attention of your supervisor separately.

Send the report on Fridays so it's an end-of-the-week treat.

Name the staff whose programs are getting attention, who helped create social media content, and so on. People often love to see their name in print (and if you're uncertain whether they would appreciate it, ask them ahead of time).

If your numbers drop dramatically (usually thanks to an algorithm change), write a couple of sentences explaining what happened. This gives just a bit of context.

Exclude mentioning retweets by bots or newspaper links to stories that are not adding to the conversation. You are generally looking for real people's engagement with your organization and its work.

**WATCH OUT!**

A weekly frequency for this report is suggested because the report takes so long to create. A weekly report is also short enough that staff can view it in five minutes. If you sent out a fully detailed report once a month, no one is going to spend twenty minutes reading it.

## NOTES

1. G2 Crowd, "Best Social Media Management Software," https://www.g2crowd .com/categories/social-media-mgmt.

2. Shawn Paul Wood, "Bad News: Negative Headlines Get Much More Attention," 2014, https://www.adweek.com/digital/bad-news-negative-headlines-get-much -more-attention.

3. Editorial, "Primer on Absolute vs. Relative Differences," *Effective Clinical Practices*, January/February 2000. http://ecp.acponline.org/janfeb00/primer.htm.

4. StackExchange, "Permanently Delete a Shortened Link from bit.ly," https:// webapps.stackexchange.com/questions/6531/permanently-delete-a-shortened -link-from-bit-ly.

# chapter 9

# Outside Contacts

FOR THE MOST PART, THIS CHAPTER COVERS OUTSIDE CONTACTS WHO CAN help get the word out about your organization. You will learn how to document preexisting relationships, establish new ones, and write press releases. Finally, you need to make some friends to exchange ideas with. The final guide will help you network with other marketers.

## GUIDE 59: Document Your Public Relations Contacts

**YOUR GOAL**
As long as your organization is not brand-new, your colleagues probably have already developed relationships with outside people and groups that can share news about your promotions. This knowledge may be employee-based and not formally documented. In this guide, you are going to gather that information and record it.

**DIFFICULTY LEVEL** Easy.

**TIME** Sixty minutes.

**COST** Free.

**WHAT YOU NEED TO START**
Know who in your organization might have outside contacts' information. A contact may be a reporter or other journalist, a teacher, a blogger, or someone else

who is interested in news from your organization. It's a mutually beneficial relationship for them and your organization: you give them content in exchange for the publicity.

## TOOLS
- E-mail or phone
- Place to keep the information

## WHAT YOU NEED TO KNOW
The list of outside contacts that you gather will likely be incomplete. There may be other people who can be added to it to help expand your organization's reach to the community. You will learn how to find them in Guide 61: "Find New Contacts."

## STEPS
1. Contact your colleagues via e-mail or phone to ask them if they have any outside contacts with whom they share news about the organization. Start with the department head, and then ask if there is anyone in their group who contacts outside people.
2. Once your colleague has affirmed that they have a contact, follow up to ask for the contact's information. Make sure to ask for any tips about their publication or their group's interest, what name they prefer to be addressed by (e.g., Steve instead of Steven), their contact preference, and any information about how they publicize information.
3. Gather all this data and put it into your knowledge base (Guide 13: "Personal Knowledge Base"). You can also put it in a spreadsheet (Guide 61: "Find New Contacts").
4. Let your supervisor know where this information can be found. When you're away, they may need to contact your publicity allies.

## TIPS
The staff may need some memory-jogging to help them recall who their contacts are in the community. Ask if there is a local business, church, or school that likes to hear about certain programs from your organization. Be clear that you will use this information to introduce yourself to the contact, ask the contact about his or her needs, and build up your organization's outreach base. These contacts are usually employed by a publication, or they work in a community group.

You are not looking for the contacts' personal relationships, such as people they e-mail when a particular new book comes in.

## WATCH OUT!
The worst-case scenario is that some of your colleagues are unwilling to share this information. However, since you have taken on this marketing role, you have some authority behind you in asking for their help in documenting your organization's

contact list. If you really run into resistance, ask your supervisor for the best strategies to approach these colleagues.

## GUIDE 60: Set Up Meetings

### YOUR GOAL
Which events, resources, and human interest stories are your outside contacts interested in? You want to save yourself time by only sending news that publications are interested in hearing about.

**DIFFICULTY LEVEL** Intermediate.

**TIME** Thirty minutes per meeting.

**COST** $10 per meeting.

### WHAT YOU NEED TO START
Contact information for your local journalists, bloggers, and so on.

### TOOLS
- Calendar
- Phone or e-mail
- Notebook
- Coffee money

### WHAT YOU NEED TO KNOW
Be up-front with why you are asking to meet your outside contacts. They will understand that your relationship is a form of give-and-take. You are not begging for publicity. They need your information in order to fill up space in their publication, and keep their readers informed.

### STEPS
1. Look at your list of contacts and decide who are the most influential ones (Guide 59: "Document Your Public Relations Contacts"). They are your top priority to meet. If you have time and extra coffee money, you can reach out to the others.
2. Draft your e-mail or the message that you want to convey over the phone. Go for a casual tone as opposed to a formal one.
3. The contents of the message may cover:
   a. A thank-you for their support over X time
   b. Ask to meet with them for coffee. Express a desire to put a face to their name.
   c. Suggest a general time frame for the meeting.

4. Coffee is great, since it can be fairly inexpensive and gives you an opportunity to meet on neutral ground outside of your organization.

   • You could skip coffee, but it helps to convince people to take time out of their day to talk with you.

5. You may want to bring along a colleague who specializes in the contact's area of interest (e.g., are you meeting a children's blogger? Bring a children's librarian).

6. Once you have scheduled your meeting, send a reminder the day before.

7. At the meeting, buy the coffee, introduce yourself, and then ask how the contact got into his or her line of work (this is the icebreaker). Then ask:

   a. What kind of stories are you looking for?

   b. Who are your primary audiences?

   c. How far in advance do you want to know about things? (Their answer may differ from the one your colleagues gave you.)

   d. What format should I send my materials to you (e.g., via e-mail, text document)?

   e. Are there any style guides that I should try to adhere to (e.g., March 10th vs. March 10)?

   f. Do you want pictures? If so, what kinds of images are of interest to you?

   g. Are there slow times of the year when you would like to receive a heads-up on our events to fill your publication's needs?

8. The meeting should last thirty minutes or so. Once you get back to the library, write a thank-you note.

9. Type up your notes in your personal knowledge base (Guide 13: "Personal Knowledge Base").

**TIPS**

Your outside contacts are very busy people. You want to make their lives easier by sending them content that is ready-packaged for them. That way, they are more likely to publish your materials.

If you have a professional marketing background, you may be used to writing formal "who, what, when, where, why" press releases. For small publications, they may not want this format. They just want to do a slight tweak to match their formatting needs and then pop in your content. Ask them in order to determine their needs.

This meeting is less stressful if you can go with a colleague. That way they can carry on the conversation while you are taking down notes.

You may be asked to just upload your events directly to the contact's (or the publication's) website. When I did my rounds, three publications asked me to do this instead of e-mailing them press releases.

**WATCH OUT!**

Don't get too concerned that each contact may have different formatting needs. If they are newspapers, they likely adhere to a similar style, so you can easily e-mail them in bulk. For tips on developing press releases, see Guide 62: "Press Releases."

Be prepared to be stood up. If a hot story develops suddenly, your contact may forget about their meeting with you. Make sure to carry their phone number so you can call them from the coffee shop if they are fifteen minutes late.

## GUIDE 61: Find New Contacts

**YOUR GOAL**

Does your organization have no outside contacts who can promote your resources, events, and services? Or is your target audience not being reached by your existing contacts? You can improve your chances to expand your outreach by making new public relations contacts. However, you need to know where to find them first.

**DIFFICULTY LEVEL** Intermediate.

**TIME** Two hours.

**COST** Free.

**WHAT YOU NEED TO START**

Patience to dig through search results.

**TOOLS**
- E-mail or phone
- Spreadsheet

**WHAT YOU NEED TO KNOW**

You will likely find more potential contacts than you can manage all by yourself. Don't try to contact them all. Prioritize your time.

**STEPS**

1. Set up a simple spreadsheet to track your efforts.
2. Use these columns:
    a. Organization Name
    b. Contact Name
    c. E-Mail/Phone
    d. Audience
    e. Interests
    f. How Often to Contact
    g. Notes

3. Check these places for new contact opportunities:
   - Newspapers
   - Local bloggers
     - Do a web search for [your town name] and blog (e.g., parenting blog, local entertainment scene blog, or book reviewer).
   - Local Instagrammers
     - Check the tags for your town, your organization, and location tags.
   - Local homegrown news sites (e.g., Patch.com, DailyVoice.com)
   - Public access TV
   - Radio
   - PTO boards and parenting groups
   - Homeschool groups
   - Realtors

4. Look for these qualities in your potential contacts: they update regularly, have a local and sizable audience, and an upbeat attitude.

5. Note your leads and prioritize them in your spreadsheet. Include what you suspect about the contact's audience; in particular, its demographics and interests.
   - Finding these leads now will make it easier to later help a colleague find a particular audience for focused marketing needs.

6. Contact your top leads by introducing yourself, outline how you can help them fulfill their constant content needs, and find out if they would be interested in talking more.

7. Once you have an affirmative response, ask them about their audience, what they want to hear about from you, and how often you may send them information. Add all this to your spreadsheet.

8. If they are not interested, thank them for their time and invite them to contact you if an opportunity comes up later.

## TIPS

Check the newspapers regularly for editor and journalist hires and leaves. Then contact them to offer them congratulations or wish them well.

Realtors like to post about local happenings and community offerings in order to make the area look more attractive to prospective home buyers. Their posts may be shared or liked hundreds of times. When I checked those postings, it looked like they were mostly aimed at other realtors but getting your name out there in such a good way—even if a little impersonal—can't hurt.

If this is a more informal relationship (especially with bloggers), you can conduct most of your relationship over the phone or via e-mail.

**WATCH OUT!**

Many online-only publications may want you to upload event postings on their website yourself. You can't do a "send one e-mail to all your PR contacts at once" deal with them. They'll delete it if you will not do the work for them.

In these cases, consider carefully what you want to share with them. If they are very niche-oriented, they may not be worth your time for most items. However, that one time you are promoting cat yoga, they might be the local voice to amplify your event. So don't burn your bridges!

## GUIDE 62: Press Releases

**YOUR GOAL**

Now that you have your public relations contacts, you need to get together a template so you can send them timely press releases.

**DIFFICULTY LEVEL** Intermediate.

**TIME** Thirty minutes.

**COST** Free.

**WHAT YOU NEED TO START**

You should have completed your assessment of your organization's current contacts (Guide 59: "Document Your Public Relations Contacts") and even found some new ones (Guide 61: "Find New Contacts").

**TOOLS**

- Word-processing software
- Your organization's logo if available

**WHAT YOU NEED TO KNOW**

Press releases are like resumes and CVs—everyone has a different style! Use this guide as a starting point and adjust as necessary.

**STEPS**

*The Template*

1. In the top left of your document, insert your organization's logo if you have one. Size it down to about an inch wide.

2. Under that, write the state of your press release: FOR IMMEDIATE RELEASE or EMBARGOED UNTIL xx/xx/xxxx (if it is time-specific, specify the time when it can go live).

3. Next, write the name, title, and contact information of the person who can answer questions about the press release. This may be you or the colleague who is responsible for the resource, service, or event.

4. Write the title of the press release in bold, and center it two lines down. For a template, just write Headline. Make sure to change it in the actual press release when the time comes.

5. One line down, left-align your text, and in bold, write the name of your town and city followed by a colon or em-dash.

6. Go down a few lines and then write in bold *About [Your Organization]*. Write some boilerplate text that will be included on every press release: your mission statement, an impressive stat (e.g., most visitors in the state), and your website URL. This material needs to be positive and informational. You don't know if the person who gets your press release will be familiar with your organization.

7. You can save this document at this point as a blank press release template.

### The Body Text

1. Next to your town name and under the headline, start writing the body text for this release.

2. Your press release needs to follow a "reverse pyramid" design. The most important information (who, what, where, when, and why) goes in the first paragraph. Keep your sentences short and to the point.

3. Depending on the publication the press release is going to, you may want to include eye-catching quotes and highlight the best information with bullet points for easier scanability.

4. If you have talked with your contacts, you may have an idea of their formatting (e.g., use periods in "p.m." or not). Try to make their lives easier by using their preferred formatting.
   - If you are mass-sending your press release to more than one outlet, they could each have a different format.
   - Depending on the amount of time you have available to you, you can customize each press release, or just try to stick to a middle ground which is applicable to most outlets.

5. Keep your tone to the point and friendly. You are not writing investigative journalism here, so there is no need for heavy emotional pull. Be careful not to use too much over-the-top marketing speak either. Write in the same direct way that the publication uses.

6. Only write a few paragraphs at most. Print space is expensive, so your piece will likely only have a couple of paragraphs on average. Longer pieces may appear on the Web.

### The E-Mail

1. Attach your press release to your e-mail. If you have more than one press release to send out, each one goes in a separate document.

2. If you are including photos, attach large, high-quality versions of them. Photos copied from a website will likely be too small for print.

3. If this is a mass send to several publishers, make sure to blind carbon copy (BCC) their e-mail addresses.

   - If you have the ability, you could try to set up a mail merge to help you customize e-mails so that each person gets their name included in the message.

4. The subject line I use is just [Organization Name] PR for Week of [date]. You could try more enticing subject lines, or ones that hint at the items in the press release.

5. In the e-mail's body text, include at least an idea about what press release you are sending that week. If you can make a connection between local or national events or seasonal interest (e.g., Spring Break) and your press release, write that in. Overall, be snappy, for they are busy people.

6. Note the priority order of the press releases if there is more than one. Which one do you really want to publicize?

7. Include captions for your photos. Check the publications to see how they usually write them out. If a photo has a photographer who needs to be attributed, include that in the e-mail *and* in the file name of the photo (e.g., mona_lisa_photo_by_leonardo.jpg).

8. If your press release needs to be embargoed until a particular date, mention that in bold within the e-mail's body text.

### Resources

- Nancy Dowd and Mary Evangeliste, *Bite-Sized Marketing: Realistic Solutions for the Overworked Librarian*
- Russel D. James and Peter J. Wosh, eds., *Public Relations and Marketing for Archives: A How-to-Do-It Manual*

### TIPS

You should send press releases only to people who are interested in them. Unsolicited e-mails will get you routed to the spam box.

Other people in your organization can write press releases but try to send them all out through you. This establishes your credibility and reputation not only within your organization, but in the community.

Read some of the articles released by your press outlets. How do they write? What can you mimic? You want to make your press release as easy to read as possible, and sometimes get it copied in full into the publication.

You can try out new press release layouts. A more traditional corporate one has clearly marked "who, what, when, where, and why." Local news outlets may want ones that are more web-friendly and informal.

After you write a few press releases, you will get faster at writing them.

**WATCH OUT!**

Just because you point out repeatedly that your press release is embargoed doesn't mean that the outlet will not release it early. This can happen to anyone. If that happens, try to make amends as quickly on your end so as not to disappoint readers. If there was a URL in your press release directing people to a website, set up a temporary version of that page that says something about it going live at the time you actually wanted the announcement to go out.

Then follow up with your contact to ask them how they want to mark embargoed press releases better in the future. Remember: you are trying not to burn your bridges here. You still want to reach their audience.

## GUIDE 63: Other Press Releases to Send

Aside from your regularly scheduled press releases, you should alert your outside contacts whenever your organization is doing something that connects with national news, holidays, or fun activities. For each of these examples, make sure to clearly connect it to the larger community interest.

### NATIONAL EVENTS AND STORIES

What is going on in the national news? What stories are being talked about around the water cooler in your building? If your organization's response is to host an event, highlight it in a press release. Sample national news events include:

- How to respond to a national tragedy
- Specific health trends (e.g., the opioid epidemic)
- Solar eclipse
- Holidays and unusual days (e.g., a program on superstitions held just before Friday the 13th)

### LOCAL EVENTS

The micro-level of marking, celebrating, and participating in local events is great for hometown-focused reporting.

- Your organization is entering a float in the local parade
- A big anniversary for the town or institution
- Staff are participating in a marathon to raise awareness for [topic]
- Things to do with kids over a school holiday break

## PHOTO OPPORTUNITIES

Reporters love good photo opportunities. If you are hosting something unusual and splashy, give the reporter a heads-up. This can tie into the national news items (e.g., solar eclipse) or local news (e.g., summer reading). Photos of kids having fun is an easy front-page filler for newspapers on slow news days. These events are typically not ones associated with the general hubbub of your organization:

- Special festivals like a maker's fair
- Fire trucks
- Petting zoo
- Events that encourage participants to dress up (e.g., a dance party or murder mystery)

Just be mindful to take and share photos within your photography policy (Guide 31: "Photography Policies").

## GUIDE 64: One-Off Press Releases

### YOUR GOAL

Are you launching a new service? Or hosting a showing of a big TV event? These are great opportunities to try and get press coverage for unusual happenings.

### DIFFICULTY LEVEL Easy.

### TIME Thirty minutes.

### COST Free.

### WHAT YOU NEED TO START

You'll need to know well ahead of time when new services, resources, or special events will occur. Ideally, you should know which public relations contact may be interested in running a piece on it.

### TOOLS

- Word-processing tool
- Press release template

### WHAT YOU NEED TO KNOW

You should know weeks in advance when your organization is going to launch a new service or resource or if there will be a special event. You may need to ask colleagues directly if they will be doing anything to capitalize on that occasion (e.g., total eclipse).

## STEPS

1. Open up your press release template (Guide 62: "Press Releases"). Start writing what is interesting, useful, and exciting about your topic.

2. Read over your text to see if it sounds like something that is newsworthy. Will this catch a reader's eye? Does it fulfill a need? Does it capitalize on a national trend?

3. Ask the colleague responsible for this new service/resource/event to read over the press release. Is there anything missing?

4. When you feel that your press release is as enticing as possible, send it to your contact. Keep your e-mail message short. Say up-front that this press release is a little unusual, but will interest their readers because . . .

## TIPS

Local newspapers and event bloggers are very interested in happenings surrounding holidays and school breaks.

Keep tabs on who runs these one-off press releases in their publication. If they showed interest once, they may do so again. If you have a good relationship with your contact, ask them directly what they are looking for.

If you are hosting a variety of "kids out of school" programs, send them out as one press release unless one is really special. A special program would be "Neil deGrasse Tyson is coming to your event," or a concert special.

## WATCH OUT!

If you are working with a colleague on this one-off press release, stress that there is no guarantee that anyone will pick up this topic. Many publications are only interested in events.

## GUIDE 65: Networking

If you are the sole person in charge of marketing for your organization, it can feel pretty lonely. No one else may understand your frustrations, or love geeking out over increased website visits, or puzzle over why e-mail opens are down lately. The solution is to network and meet your fellow marketers at other libraries.

## LOCAL MARKETERS

Shortly after being named my library's publicity manager, I received an e-mail from Kate Petrov, the public relations officer at Greenwich Library—just down the road. She invited me to come meet with her. Over that hour, she encouraged me to ask her questions about how to handle marketing for a public library, how she structured her team, and talked about the opportunities and challenges of marketing. She even gave me recommendations for books to help get me up to speed.

I've also met or e-mailed with other marketers from other local libraries. We don't have county-level library systems in Connecticut, just town ones, so we often work alone or in very small teams. The only way for us to learn from each other is to reach out directly. I have a data-sharing relationship with another library, so we can puzzle out e-mail engagement patterns together. If either one of us sees a big drop in opens which we can't explain away by holidays, sporting events, or vacations, we reach out to the other to see if they saw the same thing.

## ROUNDTABLES

Try to connect with local marketers by joining a roundtable. This may mean forming a marketing-only group or visiting other ones. At a recent adult programming roundtable, I realized that I could offer suggestions to the attendees. They asked how they could do a better job of promoting author events. I gave examples of what had worked for me, as well as which social media trends to engage in.

## ONLINE MARKETERS

For day-to-day queries and ideas, it is helpful to join online marketing groups. While I am in some LinkedIn groups, their commercial ideas don't always translate well to nonprofits. Groups that are focused on libraries and archives marketing have been more helpful. These are the Facebook groups which I find engaging:

- Library Marketing and Outreach (LMaO) https://www.facebook.com/groups/acrl.lmao
- Library Marketing and Communications Conference https://www.facebook.com/groups/LMCC.Discussion.Group
- The Shareable Clique: Viral Content for Libraries https://www.facebook.com/groups/ShareableClique

You can look for other marketers on social media, too. In your keyword search for them, look for words like *library, archive, museum, communications, marketer, publicity, manager.*

*chapter* 10

# Bonus Insights

THE COLLECTIONS OF TIPS OFFERED IN THIS CHAPTER DON'T FIT INTO ANY other category. You will learn tips on social media, handling complaints and apologizing, how to order items, and how to protect your accounts with two-factor authentication. Each guide will help you do your job more effectively.

## GUIDE 66: Google My Business

**YOUR GOAL**
How do you control your organization's information and profile on Google? To have any say in it, you need to claim your Google My Business profile.

**DIFFICULTY LEVEL** Intermediate.

**TIME** Sixty minutes.

**COST** Free.

**WHAT YOU NEED TO START**
A Google account, a (non-P.O. Box) physical mailing address, and the authority to represent your organization to Google.

**TOOLS**
- Access to Google
- Physical mailing address

**WHAT YOU NEED TO KNOW**

Google My Business (GMB) listings are shown in search results and in Google Maps, which is very convenient for users. The downside for your organization is that users won't need to visit your website to learn basic information like your hours since it shows up in Google's results. This removes opportunities for users to serendipitously learn of other offerings that appear on your website.

The best way to influence what Google shares about your organization is to claim your GMB profile so you have some say in what information they share with searchers. In exchange, you are given some data about how people are discovering your organization through their search engine.

The steps below are approximate, since the directions will change.

**STEPS**

1. Go to https://google.com/business and create an account.

2. Log in with your Google account and follow the instructions to start claiming your business.

3. You may not be able to finalize your account for a few weeks until you get a postcard in the mail which has a code you need to input. Postcard verification is the most common method.

4. Once your account has been verified with the code from the postcard, you can add your location(s).

5. Fill out all the fields for your location. These include phone number, address, photos, operating hours, and setting your future holiday closing hours.

**TIPS**

Set a regular time each month to pull your listing's stats from the Insights section. The results only show for the last three months. The numbers disappear at the end of every quarter (March, June, September, and December). There is no export function or way to look at historical numbers at this time. You can learn whether people found your organization on Google.com or within Google Maps, keywords people use to look up your organization, and how users tried to reach you -- by asking for directions or calling.

Any Google user may leave a rating, review, or question for your location. You should set up notifications so you can respond in a timely fashion to all interactions. If there is a negative comment, see Guide 67: "Handling Complaints" for strategies on how to respond.

Refresh your photos every now and then.

Use all the other features that you can manage within GMB. Google Posts allows you to highlight an item to show below your GMB profile in search results. Use this space to promote an upcoming event or to highlight a resource. Track the reviews and clicks over time to see which of your post types are most successful.

**WATCH OUT!**
Talk with your supervisor about the impact of GMB on your website's stats. People are more likely to find simple information about your organization (address, hours) from a quick search engine search than from hunting for the information on your About page. If possible, capture the search stats from GMB to accompany your website's other logged data.

Note: Even if you don't create a GMB account which includes your hours, Google may still pull the data off your website or another resource anyway.

Sometimes Google will get your organization's name wrong. You can report it, but there is no guarantee they will correct it. Your best chance is to go to the Google Forums and ask for help correcting the problem.[1]

## GUIDE 67: Handling Complaints

**YOUR GOAL**
Uh-oh. It's the dreaded complaint or negative comment. The unhappy user's words may come in via the Web, phone, or e-mail. Here are some strategies to help you handle this situation without turning it into a public relations disaster.

**DIFFICULTY LEVEL** Hard.

**TIME** Sixty minutes.

**COST** Free.

**WHAT YOU NEED TO START**
Check your organization's policies to see if someone has already done the legwork on how to handle complaints. It may be in a section on social media.

**TOOLS**
  • Organizational policy
  • Supervisor for backup

**WHAT YOU NEED TO KNOW**
This guide is timed at an hour because that gives you time to investigate the complaint, discuss responses with the appropriate people, and then respond to it. Handling negative comments is a high-stress situation that needs to be handled with a deft touch.

**STEPS**
  1. Once you become aware of the complaint, notify your supervisor about the situation as soon as possible. Time is of the essence in handling complaints.

2. Gather information regarding the issue if one is specified in the user's comment. You want to know who was involved and any staff knowledge about the issue.

3. How delicate is the situation with this particular user?

   a. Is the person going to scream at you on every social media account and at the next town hall meeting?

   b. Or would a phone call to the user suffice?

4. If the issue is about a . . .

   a. Staff member: alert their supervisor.

   b. Resource: if it's a censorship issue, consult your policies.

   c. Technical issue: connect the user with help right away.

   d. Social/ethical concern: you may need an internal response team to develop a reply.

   e. Legal: follow your policy, which is likely to alert the administration.

   f. Political: consult with your supervisor, and it may require an internal response team to develop a reply.

5. Is the issue something that can be fixed?

   a. If yes, try to make it right.

   b. If no, draft a statement explaining why.

6. Other response options:

   a. Ignore the complaint. This may or may not backfire, depending on how determined the person is on being acknowledged.

   b. Delete the comment. An ideal policy would include a notice that you reserve the right to delete anything that contains slurs, curse words, or threatens harm/violence. In case of threats, your organization should contact your local law enforcement agency.

7. Decide if you respond differently to a complaint from a local user versus someone elsewhere in the world.

   • Local users may warrant a response, while someone just throwing complaints out at random accounts online may not merit a response. By replying, you may draw their attention again.

8. Start drafting your response to the situation. Run it past your supervisor and anyone else who should have a say in it.

9. Decide whether to respond publicly or reach out privately to the person.

   a. Pros of responding publicly: If the complaint is not justified, you can correct a misconception or misunderstanding. The person may even thank you.

   b. Cons of responding publicly: The person may react even more strongly, with numerous follow-up posts. At this point, you're likely drawing attention from other users. If you don't maintain a courteous and helpful tone, you can come out looking very badly.

    c. Pros of responding privately: Personal details about the user are not exposed on an open forum.

    d. Cons of responding privately: If you don't post something along the lines of "I have sent you a direct message" to the public comment, it can look like you are ignoring the user, which may look bad.

10. Tips on how to respond:

    a. In most situations, a thoughtful apology is a good way to start the conversation.

    b. Be courteous.

    c. Avoid judgmental words.

    d. A joking tone or response to serious issues can be taken as dismissive.

11. Try to take the discussion off-line if it's happening on social media or your website. You will see that airports and cable companies are always directing people to contact them at X to discuss their concern in detail. Do the same whether it is in-person, phone, or e-mail.

12. Understand that some people cannot be satisfied. When it gets to this level, someone higher up in the organization should take care of the situation. Your job is to notice the trouble and bring it to someone else's attention if the situation warrants it.

13. Consider documenting any complaints that require this level of consideration. Small issues like a broken website link can be addressed quickly. For anything that requires a large group effort in addressing the concern, this should be noted somewhere, especially if you run into someone who begins harassing your organization.

## TIPS

If a complaint is on Facebook, you are often forced to respond, since the platform promotes posts based on users' activity and engagement with a post and comments.

If a complaint is on Twitter, Instagram, or YouTube, you may be better served by ignoring it. Retweets are very easy to share and can get widespread attention fast. At the same time, if the complaint is very small, the only person who will likely see it is the user and their followers. However, if the user is an active community member, this is not the route to risk!

## WATCH OUT!

Any written correspondence may be posted online, so tread carefully.

One of the worst-case scenarios is for your organization to get targeted for repeated Freedom of Information Act (FOIA) requests. Some libraries and local organizations have seen these turn into lawsuits. The cost of handling these situations can run into hundreds of thousands of dollars.

If your organization becomes subject to repetitive online harassment, seek legal counsel.

If you are seeing a serious lapse in judgment or a repeating pattern of behavior that reflects badly on your organization from a staff member, consider bringing it up with your supervisor. Come prepared to explain what you have witnessed, why it is troubling, your suggestions for how to improve it, and maybe a log detailing when you witnessed this behavior. Note that this is going to be a high-stress situation. You may not get the desired outcome that will stop the behavior.

## GUIDE 68: How to Apologize

### YOUR GOAL
Your organization has made a serious mistake and you need to apologize to a user. How do you do so without making the situation worse?

### DIFFICULTY LEVEL Hard.

### TIME Sixty minutes.

### COST Free.

### WHAT YOU NEED TO START
You need to know when an apology is warranted.

### TOOLS
- Access to a communication tool that the user also has access to so that they may read your response.

### WHAT YOU NEED TO KNOW
What an authentic apology looks like will evolve over time. This text provides you with guidance on how to respond, but you may want to do a web search for recent public apologies and see how the commenters responded to them. The public commentary will often point out why they found the apology ineffective if not outright making the situation worse. Try to avoid the missteps commenters describe.

### STEPS
1. You discover that a situation has arisen where your organization needs to make a sincere apology. What this situation looks like will depend entirely on what happened. Since this is coming to your attention, it is usually made through a complaint that has been posted online.
2. The basics of a good apology should contain these elements:
   a. Acknowledge that a mistake has been made.
   b. Apologize for what happened.
   c. What will your organization do to make amends?

d. How will your organization try to do better?

e. Thank the person for bringing the issue to your attention.

3. Depending on the situation, you may invite the person to give further feedback or to get involved in improving things. For example, if someone discovers a mistake in how you are handling resource sustainability, and they are a leader in the local environment group, they may be willing to help advise or give feedback to an internal committee on the issue.

4. Try not to put the burden on the user to help you. You can ask if they would like to help, but you should understand that in many situations, you are asking nonprofessionals to do unpaid work. This is not fair. Moreover, the user may not have the expertise to teach how to correct behavior, thoughts, or bias. They just recognized a wrong.

5. Accept that sometimes an apology will not be accepted.

### TIPS

Apologies can feel very personal, especially in situations when you know a grave mistake was made. Try your best to separate your ego and feelings from the situation. Otherwise, you may worry yourself into having a bad day.

### WATCH OUT!

Sometimes someone will become even angrier after you apologize. If that happens, see the tips in Guide 67: "Handling Complaints."

## GUIDE 69: Ordering Items

Have you been tasked with getting some branded swag? There are many places to place your order locally or online. The Internet will likely provide the most competitive prices. There are a few things to keep in mind, however.

### WOULD ANYONE WANT THIS?

When you check out catalogs for swag to hand out, there is a dazzling array of items. But before you whip out that credit card, stop and think. Does anyone really want a cheap pen which never quite writes? Sure, you have something to give out, but if it's not usable, it'll cause frustration. Slow down and consider the impression you're giving your users when they are frustrated with the pen you gave them.

Think of the target audience that you want to give the swag to. Consider the context as to when you would want to give them something to keep. Is it appropriate? One of the best swag items I have ever received was lip balm at a Las Vegas conference. It was immediately useful for the dry desert environment.

### SAMPLES

To help you avoid surprises, order a sample item so you can see how the item looks, works, and feels in-person. Some vendors will send you a sample for just the cost of shipping. The sample item may have no logo or text on it, so you won't get a completely accurate idea of what the finished product looks like. The item may also have bubbles in the paint, since it was placed aside just for this free sample purpose. Talk to customer service and get it in writing that the final item will not have these imperfections.

## PRICING

When you are trying to stretch your budget, you may be tempted to order the highest quantity of pens you can find for the cheapest price. If you can, first get a sample of the pen and check it out. If the price is too good for the quantity, the pen's quality is likely to be poor.

Your printer may also charge you for a print run setup cost. This means that the cost is not just the price per item multiplied by the quantity. If you are charged for the setup cost, this may equal the entire price you were expecting to pay for just the items themselves. If you encounter this, make sure to order as many items as you can afford at once, because you will be charged the setup price every time you order. Save money and buy in bulk.

## INVOICING

Ask when you will be billed for your order. While we are used to stores and gas stations charging us immediately, an online company may not charge your credit card for weeks. If you are close to the end of the fiscal year's ordering season, this is vital information. The worst outcome is when your expensive purchase ends up billed to the wrong fiscal year's budget.

## COLORS

Professional printers require images sent to them to be in CYMK format (Guide 26: "Print Materials"). You can easily convert most images in Photoshop from screen (RBG) to print CYMK.

Read the fine print to see how many colors the printer will run. Your logo may have ten colors in it, but the printer will not go beyond four. Consider adding to your branding documents which colors are acceptable if you have to print with fewer colors (Guide 3: "Know Your Branding"). This may be easy if your logo is made up of shades of blue, green, and purple. The acceptable color for one-color prints could be any one of those three colors. Red would not work.

## IMAGES

Along with requiring images to be CYMK, you may be asked to submit a vector version. This means that the image is endlessly resizable without losing quality. Vector versions are usually made in Adobe Illustrator or Inkscape. Vector is a great thing to have, since you can use the same image and export it out at sizes ranging from a business card to a billboard. These are usually not photos, but logos or illustrations.

You may also be asked for a transparent background image. Commonly, this means that the picture is saved as a PNG and not a JPG (or JPEG). The point of this is so that your image's background is the color of the item it is printed on. You should save JPG images for printing photos on your item. Use transparent background images for logos and text.

## GUIDE 70: Update Content

### KEEP IT UP TO DATE
One part of marketing management is keeping your organization's information fresh online. This refers to not only changing out your social media headers for new campaigns, but also keeping the content online current.

### ANNUAL CONTENT AUDIT
Set aside some time each year to do a content audit of the online locations that you manage. In the most formal context, this involves creating a spreadsheet that lists the URL of every page. Then you can check off each page as you make sure that it is accurate. If possible, assign sections of the website to the department that should know the status of the services and resources listed there. You may need to stay on top of them to make sure they look it over for any changes. It's important that you keep up the pressure, since otherwise the staff will have to deal with angry users when something listed on the website no longer exists.

### PHOTOS
Were there any changes in the organization's building and grounds this year? Look for new paint jobs, bicycle racks, and furniture rearrangements. Snap a new photo of the improvements and update it where appropriate. Then add some of those new shots to your Google My Business profile (Guide 66: "Google My Business").

### PRINT
When you print a large quantity of items, they may outlast their relevance. If possible, try to recycle materials (as opposed to sending it to the landfill) that go out of date instead of going through and marking out incorrect information. By doing so, you will save staff time and keep your marketing materials looking sharp. If you are not allowed to get rid of the inaccurate items, consider covering old information with labels. The labels may be blank or have updated content.

### SIGNS
When was the last time your signs were updated? Do they use the same terminology? The same designs? In a class I taught, a student discovered that a sign printed in the mid-1990s was still sitting at their building's front desk!

## SOCIAL MEDIA

You should change out your social media headers for new campaigns throughout the year. When it's slow, consider doing seasonal changes, like raking autumn leaves in the fall. This is also a good time to weed out accounts that are no longer being used by your organization.

Don't forget to check your location's review pages on sites like Yelp, Google, and Trip Advisor. By adding new photos periodically, your account looks active and fresh. These sites, along with Google My Business and Facebook, will sometimes add new information areas for you to fill in.

## TEMPLATES

Did you have any staff or phone number changes this year? Make sure that any templates you use, like press releases, have the correct contact person on them. Likewise, if your boilerplate boasts a number (e.g., visitors, circulation), update it with the most recent data.

## WEBSITES

If part of your job is to manage the organization's website, get staff to fill you in on any changes made in the organization. These may involve new services or resources (e.g., databases), retired services, or moving resources to a new location. The best way to handle this is to regularly remind staff of the importance of letting you know about changes in the building and services. You also just need to keep your ear open as to what is happening. People may forget to tell you that they got rid of the shredder.

## GUIDE 71: Social Media Tips

## ACCESSIBILITY

Twitter popularized the use of hashtags to tag your content in order to make it easier to find in a search. Adrian Roselli, who develops accessible web interfaces, points out that hashtags need to be written in CamelCase;[2] that is, the first letter of each word in the hashtag needs to be capitalized. Moreover, when a screen reader reads aloud the hashtag, it will do so as separate words. Your visually impaired followers will thank you.

Twitter also allows you to describe images from within their web interface and some apps. Try to write descriptions that are meaningful. Instead of saying "picture of a graph," explain what is significant about that graph. Why did you include it in your tweet? What should people notice? Add that to the description. You may need to go into your Twitter settings to turn on this feature.

## LOCATION TAGS

You should include location tags in your organization's social media posts as appropriate. This is more useful on Instagram than on Facebook. Then people browsing your local area's location tags will see your posts even if they don't follow you. With any luck, users will tag your location as well, so you can then look at what they're saying about your organization.

## VIDEO

Video content has seen exponential growth on the Web. Moreover, Facebook weighs video uploaded to its platform more favorably than other content types.[3] What does this mean for your organization? You should create more videos and upload them. While high-quality productions are nice, you can get away with using your smartphone's camera. You should invest in a smartphone adapter so you can attach your phone to a tripod, and thus avoid shaky camera movements.

While it is tempting to create a video archive of all of your uploaded content so they are all in one place (e.g., YouTube), you will need to do extra work to format the video for each platform. If you use your smartphone, you should film using the camera app and not a social media app. Then you can post the video on multiple platforms without degrading its quality. If you had filmed the video in Instagram first, the quality is lower than if you had used your normal camera app.

## SOCIAL MEDIA POLICIES

You should develop social media policies ahead of time so you know how to handle trying situations easily and with consistency (Guide 67: "Handling Complaints"). While you cannot plan for every situation, you can get a head start by answering these questions:

- Will you allow profanity or hateful or phobic comments to stay on your posts?
- How do you handle trolling of your account?
- What do you mean by "trolling"?
- What steps do you take when someone breaks your behavior policy for your page?
- At what point do you block someone?
- When you block someone, do you tell them so first?
- How can a blocked user ask to be reinstated?

Since the best web etiquette changes over time, do a web search for recently updated policies for ideas. Check out the policies of other cultural organizations that may have similar concerns to your own.

Note: There have been lawsuits about whether public figures can block users from viewing their accounts. The complainants cite that their First Amendment rights have been violated. Consult a lawyer to make sure your social media policy stays within the law.

## BUSINESS ACCOUNTS

If possible, try to claim an organization or business account on your social media platforms. These accounts usually give you better analytics, may add a verification badge to give your account more authority, and give you better control of your organization's presence on that platform. For instance, if you find an auto-generated account for an old location, having a verified business account may help you in getting the other account shut down.

## CURATE LISTS

On some platforms, you can add accounts you follow to lists. These lists may or may not be public. They are useful when you use a tool like Tweetdeck or Hootsuite. Then you can keep an eye on what users in different categories are interested in.

For instance, if you add all users who self-identify as local residents (check their profile), then you can add them to a private list. Within your social media manager of choice, you can then have a stream of just local residents' posts. If they are all chatting about the upcoming town festival, you may score engagement points by posting about the festival in some way too. This example can raise privacy concerns, so use it as suitable to your organization's policies.

## SCHEDULING POSTS

Save yourself some sanity by scheduling your posts in advance. Then you can go on vacation without worrying that your social media accounts will go silent while you are away. Just be sure to assign someone the task of checking each day for any comments that need to be dealt with.

I have a set time each week when I create posts and then schedule them across platforms that allow it. I gather ideas for that week's social media posts in my project management software throughout the week. Additionally, I check my yearlong social media calendar for ideas on what to post about this coming week (Guide 30: "Calendars to Develop"). Then I note in my social media tracking calendar what platform I am posting to, a line about what the content is about, and the date/time.

Note: If a major national tragedy occurs, you may need to cancel your scheduled posts for that day. While everyone is reeling, the last thing they need is your organization chirping about National Puppy Day. It comes across as tone-deaf.

## CLAIM YOUR USERNAME

There are more wannabe "next big thing" websites going online every day. You cannot keep track of them all. But pay attention when you see a new platform mentioned more than a few times. If it seems like it would fit your organization, go ahead and grab your username. Add your logo, and maybe add a note in the bio that this account belongs to your organization. Then if you need to use that platform in the future, you already have your username claimed and ready to go. You want your users to find you on whatever platform they go to next, so claim your name and make it easy for them to find you. This also helps deter others from impersonating your organization. Just make sure to document this account in your personal knowledge base along with your account log-in information (Guide 13: "Personal Knowledge Base").

## RETIRING AN ACCOUNT

The time may come when a social media platform is no longer relevant for your users or your needs. In these cases, you need to decide how to retire the account. Will you delete it? Will you put it on hiatus? If you delete an account, you lose your username and someone else may be able to grab it later. In both cases, try to export out your content. What will you do with it? Who knows! But you put all that effort into it.

Whether you delete or retire the account, let your followers know ahead of time. Many platforms do not show posts in chronological order, so your users may not see the message before you abandon ship. If you are putting the account on hiatus, change the bio to say that this account is no longer being updated. Direct them to the platform where you are now active.

Note: There may be government or larger institutional policies that dictate what needs to happen to old accounts. Your posts may be part of an official record which needs to be maintained.

## GUIDE 72: Two-Factor Authentication

When you log into most sites, only a username and password are keeping you from accessing the account. They're also the only things keeping bad guys out. The rise of two-factor authentication (2FA) helps add a layer of protection between your personal data and anyone else. The basic concept is that you still have your username and password, but something else is also needed for you to log in. This other item is often a passcode. This protection is often shared by SMS text messages, an authentication app, or a list of passcodes previously copied down from the website when two-factor authentication was enabled. Either way, each code can only be used once. There are also physical authentication methods like keys and USB drives, and biometric ones like fingerprints or iris scanners.

Warning: If you lose access to the passcode authentication method, you have lost access to the site. This is often unrecoverable.

Two-factor authentication is not foolproof. If someone else gains access to your passcode, they can get into the site. SMS is the weakest 2FA method, since phone numbers can be spoofed.[4] So if you use an authentication app, make sure your phone also has a lock method (password, biometric, pattern, or code).

Adding 2FA adds a barrier to access, so it is strongly recommended to enable it on all your accounts. You are not only protecting yourself and your organization's data, but also any patron data that may be accessible from that account. Visit Two Factor Auth for an updated list of sites that support 2FA (https://twofactorauth.org).

**NOTES**

1. Google, "Google Product Forums," https://productforums.google.com/forum.

2. Adrian Roselli, "Improving Your Tweet Accessibility," 2018, http://adrianroselli .com/2018/01/improving-your-tweet-accessibility.html.

3. Alfred Lua, "Decoding the Facebook Algorithm: A Fully Up-to-Date List of the Algorithm Factors and Changes," 2018, https://blog.bufferapp.com/facebook -news-feed-algorithm.

4. Andy Greenberg, "So Hey, You Should Stop Using Texts for Two-Factor Authenti- cation," 2016, https://www.wired.com/2016/06/hey-stop-using-texts-two-factor -authentication.

# index